Identifying Chincoteague Ponies 2019

Cover photo taken May 29, 2018.

From right to left: Tornado's Legacy, A Splash of Freckles, Jigsaw's Little Miss Skeeter, Cody's Little Jigsaw Puzzle, Sweetheart (behind Skeeter and Jigsaw), Surfer Princess, Anne Bonny, Anne Bonny's 2018 foal

**Other books from
Jennie's Music Room Books**

Nicio and Cedar Fire
Legends of Two-Legs
Identifying Chincoteague Ponies [2017]
Identifying Chincoteague Ponies 2018

Jennie's Music Room Books
4241 Filmore St
Chincoteague Island, VA 23336

ISBN: 978-0-9842392-7-6

Library of Congress Control Number: 2019901836

Contents

Preface

.... 2

Ponies

Bay 4
Bay Comparison Chart 32
Bay Pinto 34
Black 110
Black Comparison Chart 118
Black Pinto 120
Buckskin 136
Buckskin Comparison Chart 154
Buckskin Pinto 156
Chestnut 172
Chestnut Comparison Chart 210
Chestnut Pinto 212
Palomino 274
Palomino Comparison Chart 286
Palomino Pinto 288

Indexes

Close Family 304
Alphabetical 320
Stallion 328
Brand 329

Last Minute Update

Thunderbolt 333

Preface

About This Book

The primary purpose of this book is to aid in the identification of individual members of the feral herd of horses known as Chincoteague ponies. These ponies reside on the southern Virginia end of Assateague Island. There is a completely separate herd at the northern Maryland end of the island know as Assateague horses. The Maryland herd is not included in this book.

This book is the work of one person. The author took the photos, drew the drawings, collected the data, formatted the pages and published the book.

There will be times when you will not be able to positively identify an individual using one resource. Animals with solid coats and very light pintos can be hard to identify. Colors appear differently depending on the season, weather, and lighting conditions. Long hair in the winter may obscure brands. Mud can cover legs. Manes blow around.

The author recommends that when in doubt, search the internet. She starts with the Chincoteague Pony Pedigree Database at chincoteaguepedigrees.com. Besides interesting geneology information, there are links to other web sites with photo galleries and band information. Another method is to post pictures and ask in any of the various Facebook pony groups, like I Love Chincoteague Ponies!

To report errors or to make suggestions for next year's book, please message me through my Facebook page - Chincoteague Pony Names.

Organization

Ponies are grouped alphabetically by color. **Bay**: Any dark colored horse with black points*. Colors range from shades of red to very dark brown. **Black**: An all black horse including points*. **Buckskin**: Any light colored horse with black/brown points*. Colors range from very light cream to yellow, tan, or gold. **Chestnut**: A reddish brown horse. Colors range from light red to deep mahogany. **Palomino**: A pale horse with white mane and tail. Colors range from cream to golden.

*points: legs, muzzle, mane and tail, and tips of ears

Each color is divided into 3 sections. **Solid:** A horse with no white markings on the body other than face and legs. **Comparison Chart**: Additional characteristics that might aid in identifying a solid horse. **Pinto**: A horse with white markings on the body other than face and legs. Any horse could have white on the face and legs.

Alphabetical by name, brand, and stallion indexes are included. The alphabetical index includes official names and popular nicknames.

There is also an family index which shows the relationships of the current living members of the herd. For more detailed pedigrees, refer to the Chincoteague Pony Pedigree Database at chincoteaguepedigrees.com.

Bay Girl

Fluffy
mare   brand: none

WITCH DOCTOR x WILD ISLAND ORCHID

Notes:

_____

_____

_____

_____

_____

_____

_____

_____

_____

_____

Bay Girl

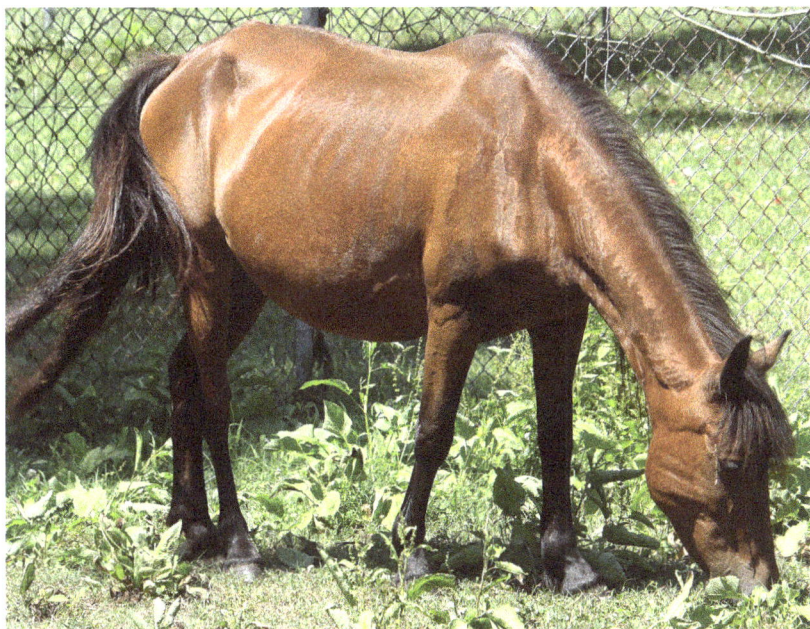

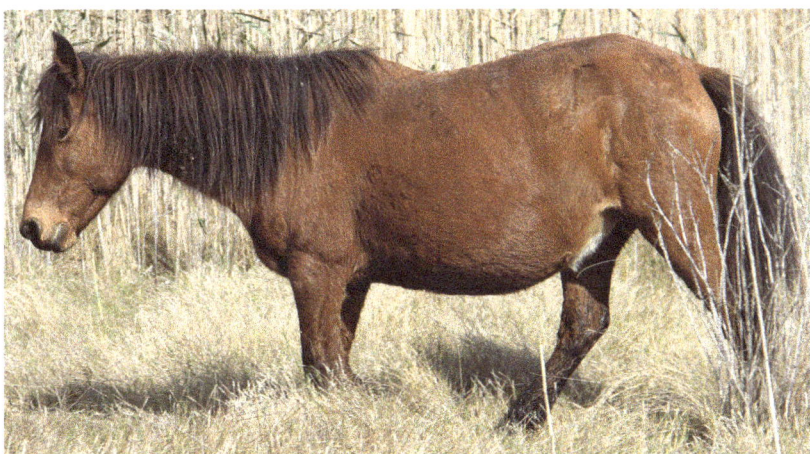

Bay

Daisey

mare   brand: none
Cinnamon Hologram x Merry Teapot's High Bid

Notes:

_____
_____
_____
_____
_____
_____

_____
_____
_____
_____

Daisey

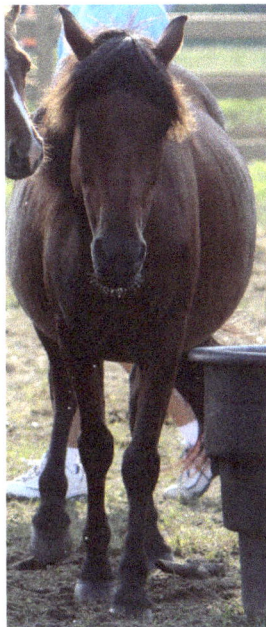

Bay

Doc's Bay Dream

mare   brand: 18
Effie's Papa Bear x Doctor Amrien

Notes:

_____

_____

_____

_____

_____

_____

_____

_____

_____

_____

Doc's Bay Dream

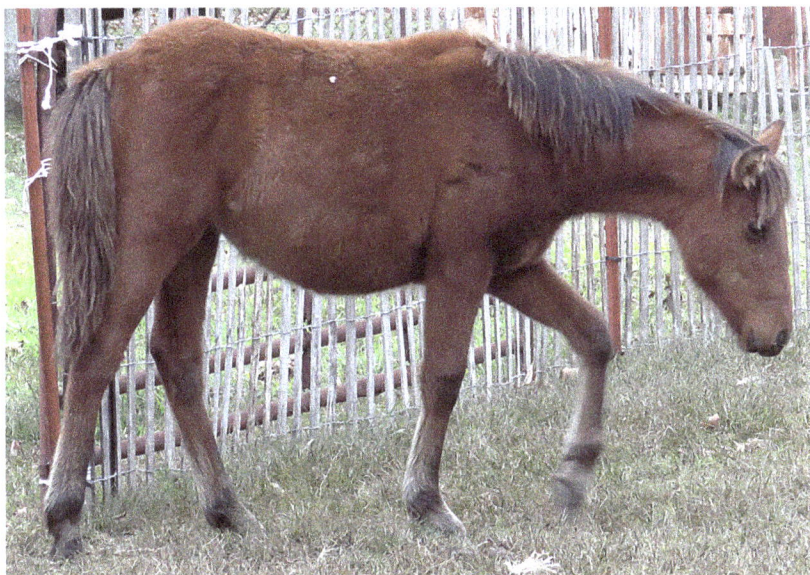

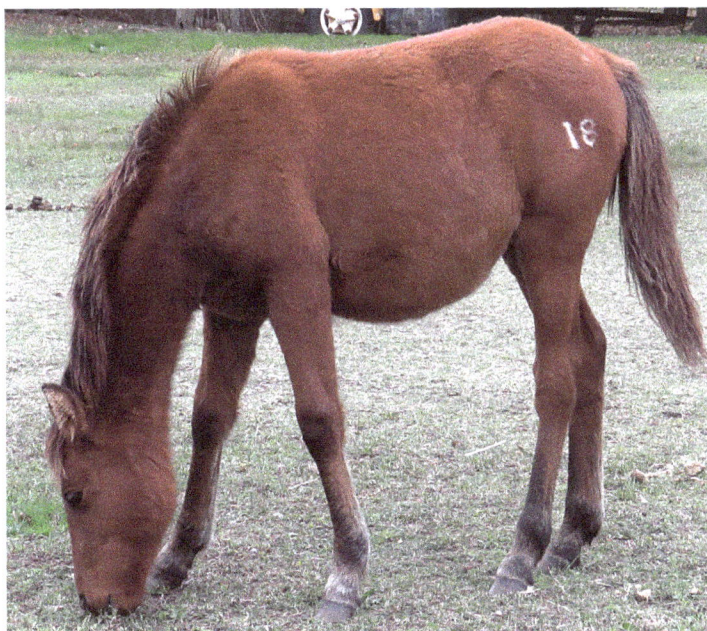

Bay

Effie's Papa Bear

Poseidon's Fury, Hoppy
stallion   brand: 07
Sockett To Me x Mermaid

Notes:

Effie's Papa Bear

Bay

Little Dolphin

Neptune
stallion   brand: 08

RAINBOW WARRIOR x LANDRIE'S GEORGIA PEACH

Notes:

Little Dolphin

Bay

Pappy's Pony

mare   brand: 03
OCEAN STAR x ISLAND STAR

Notes:

_____

_____

_____

_____

_____

_____

_____

_____

_____

_____

Pappy's Pony

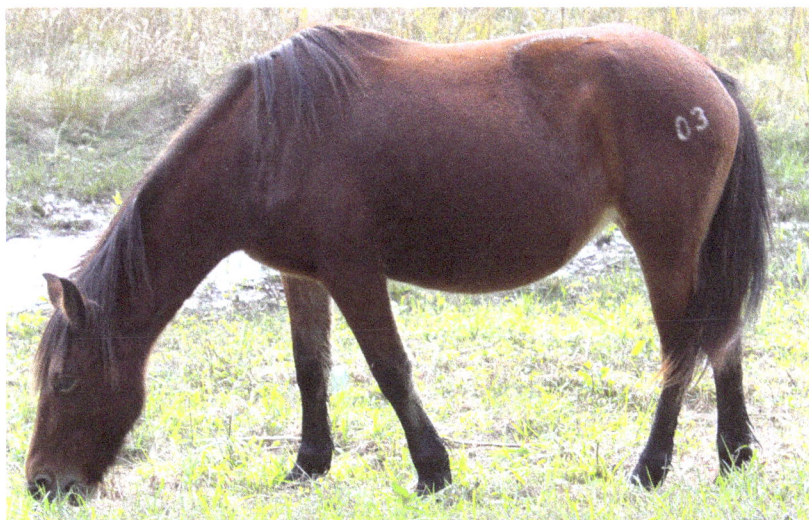

Bay

Pony Ladies' Sweet Surprise

Lady
mare   brand: 04

GUNNER'S MOON x SWEET INSPIRATION

Notes:

_____

_____

_____

_____

_____

_____

_____

_____

_____

_____

_____

Pony Ladies' Sweet Surprise

Bay

Two Teagues Taco

Taco
mare   brand: 05
Witch Doctor x Wild Island Orchid

Notes:

_____

_____

_____

_____

_____

_____

_____

_____

_____

_____

_____

Two Teagues Taco

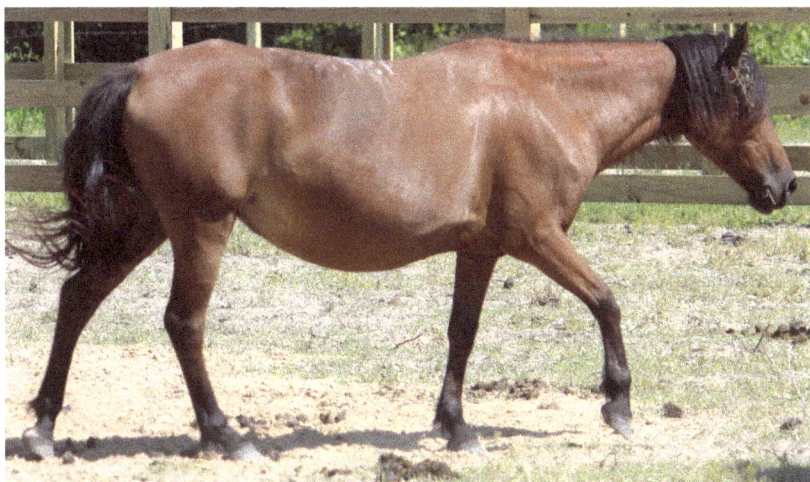

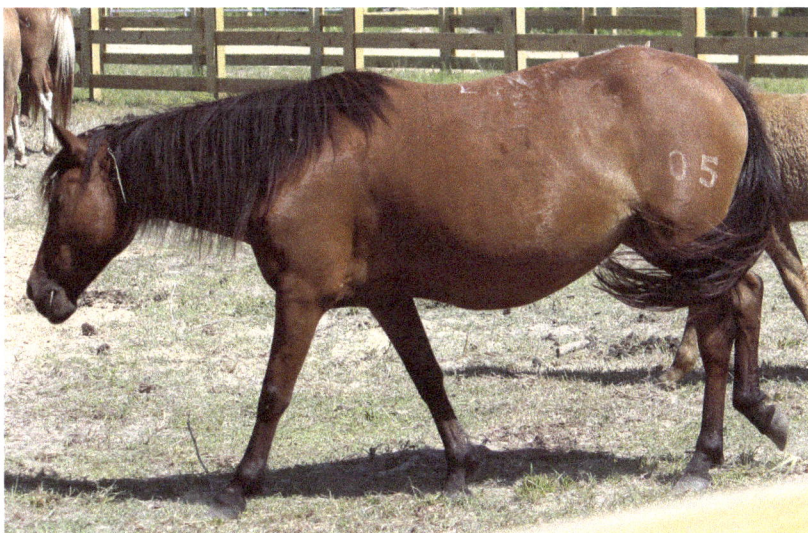

Bay

Unci

mare   brand: none
(UNKNOWN) X (UNKNOWN)

swayback

swayback

Notes:

_____

_____

_____

_____

_____

_____

_____

_____

_____

_____

_____

Unci

Bay

Jean Bonde's Bayside Angel

Angel
mare   brand: 15, partial
Sockett To Me x Leah's Bayside Angel

Notes:

Jean Bonde's Bayside Angel

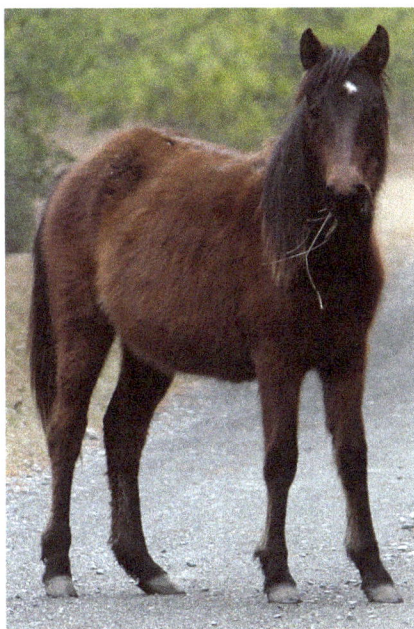

23

Bay

Leah's Bayside Angel

mare   brand: unreadable
Ocean Star x Summer Breeze

Notes:

_____

_____

_____

_____

_____

_____

_____

_____

_____

Leah's Bayside Angel

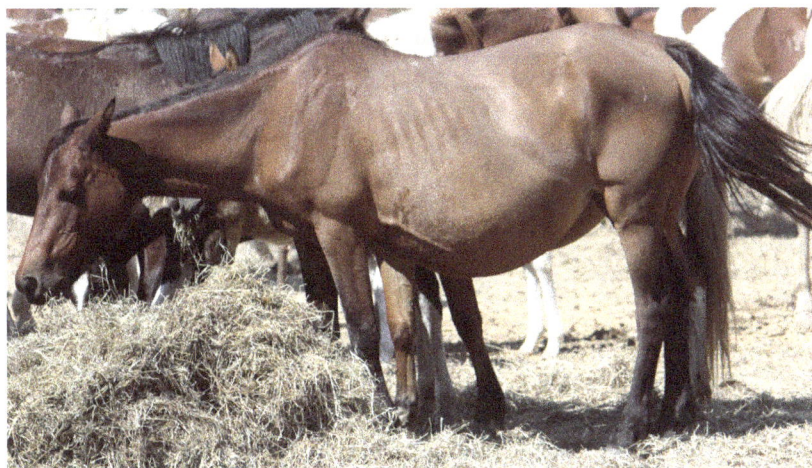

Bay

Tawny Treasure

mare   brand: 17

EFFIE'S PAPA BEAR x ISLE TREASURE

Notes:

_____

_____

_____

_____

_____

_____

_____

_____

_____

_____

Tawny Treasure

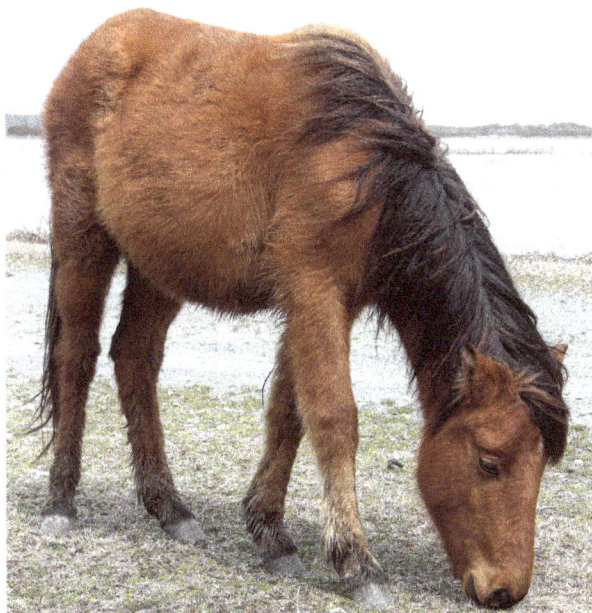

Bay

Dakota Sky's Cody Two Socks

Cody
mare   brand: 05, partial

Copper Moose x Stevenson's Dakota Sky

Notes:

_____

_____

_____

_____

_____

_____

_____

_____

_____

Dakota Sky's Cody Two Socks

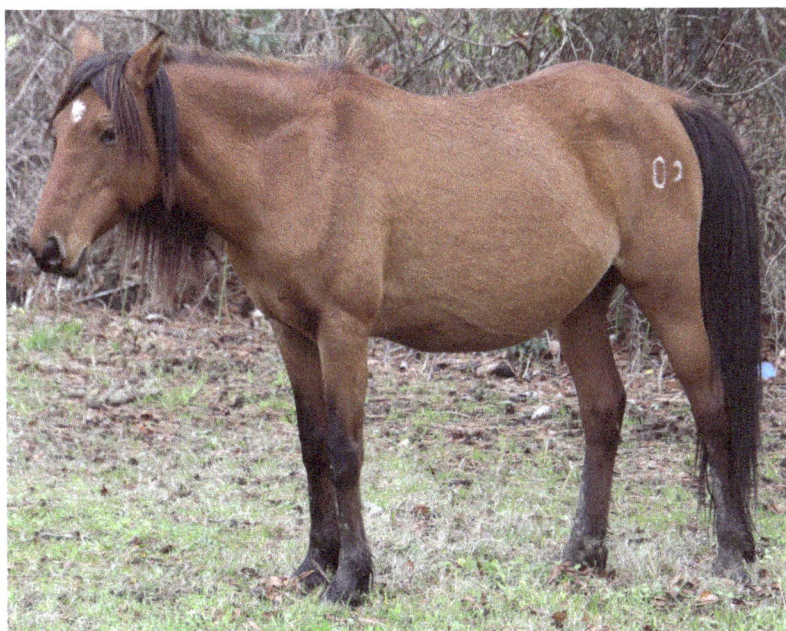

Bay

Bling Bling

mare   brand: 15

Tornado's Legacy x Unforgettable 2001

Notes:

_____

_____

_____

_____

_____

_____

_____

_____

_____

_____

Bling Bling

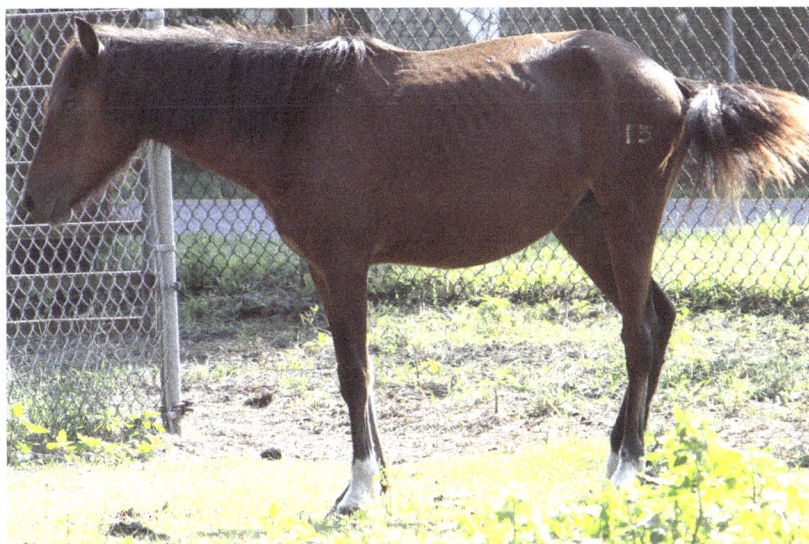

Bay Comparision Chart

Name	Pg #	Brand	Mane	Face
Bay Girl	4		left	
Bling Bling	30	15	left	star
Daisey	6		right	
Dakota Sky's Cody Two Socks	28	05, partial	right	star
Doc's Bay Dream	8	18	split	
Effie's Papa Bear	10	07	left	
Jean Bonde's Bayside Angel	22	15, partial	right	star
Leah's Bayside Angel	24	unreadable	right	star
Little Dolphin	12	08	right	
Pappy's Pony	14	03	right	
Pony Ladies' Sweet Surprise	16	04	left	
Tawny Treasure	26	17	right	star
Two Teagues Taco	18	05	left	
Unci	20		right	
Thunderbolt	333		right	

NOTES

Left & right refers to the animal's left & right.

Mane: left = falls to the left **right** = falls to the right **split** = significant portion falls on left and right

Bay Comparision Chart

Legs				Notable Details
R F	**R B**	**L F**	**L B**	
	sock	sock	sock	
	sock		sock	upper half of 5 is gone ; long forelock
				stallion; very dark mane and tail
				top of 1 in brand is obscured
				stallion; small stature
				swayback
				stallion

R F = right front **R B** = right back **L F** = left front **L B** = left back
sock = white well below the knee **stocking** = white near and above the knee

baldface = white covers most of the face **blaze** = white streak running down the length of the face **snip** = white spot on the muzzle **star** = white spot on the forehead

Bay Pinto

Rosie's Teapot

mare   brand: 13
AJAX x MOLLY'S ROSEBUD

Notes:

_____

_____

_____

_____

_____

_____

_____

_____

_____

_____

_____

Rosie's Teapot

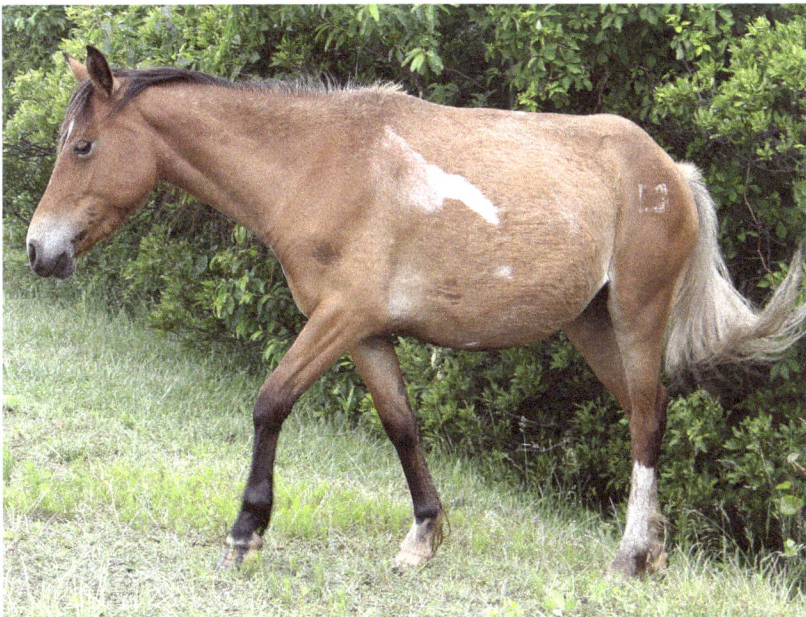

Bay Pinto

Summer Breeze

Cee Cee, Breezy
mare   brand: none
MIRACLE MAN x BINKY'S BREEZE

Notes:

_____

_____

_____

_____

_____

_____

_____

_____

_____

_____

_____

Summer Breeze

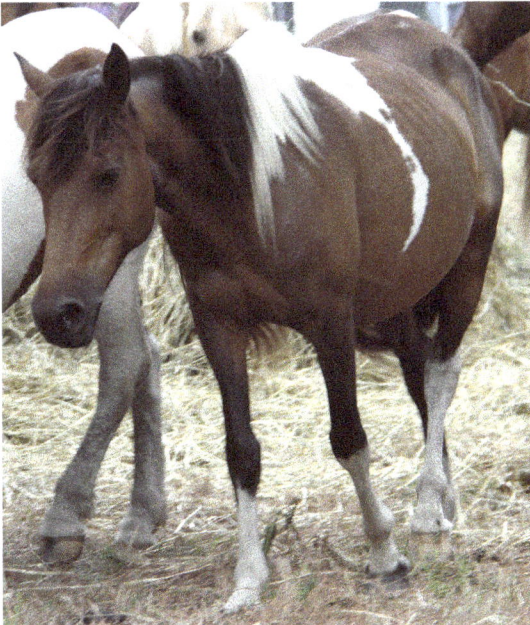

Bay Pinto

Ella of Assateague

Ella
mare   brand: 00
Cinnamon Hologram x Foxy Asset

Notes:

_____

_____

_____

_____

_____

_____

_____

_____

_____

_____

_____

Ella of Assateague

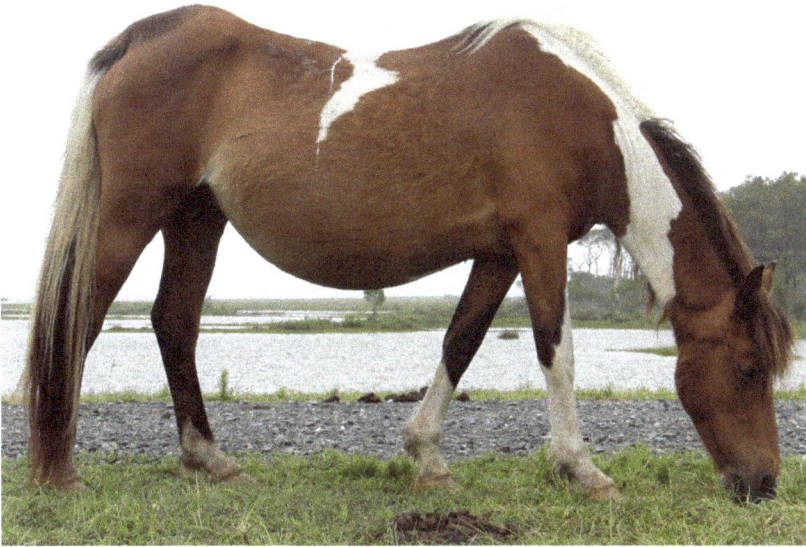

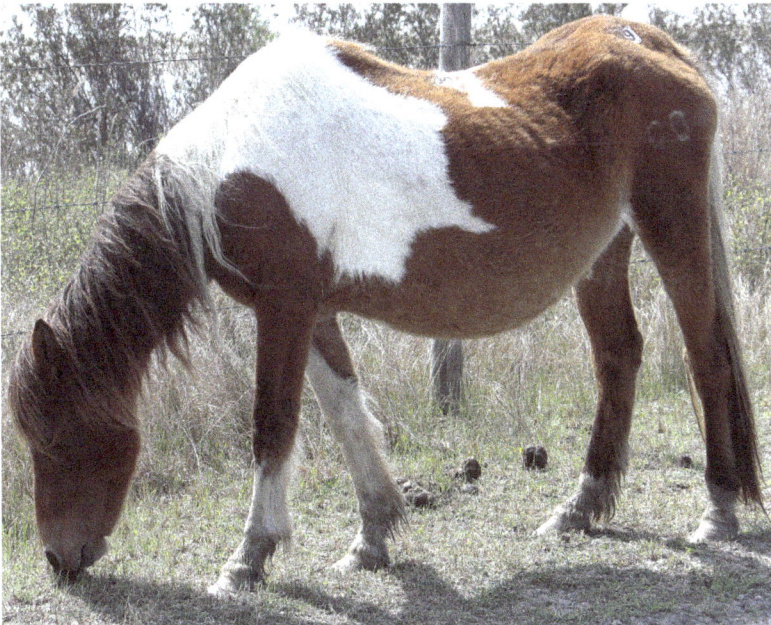

Bay Pinto

Cody's Little Jigsaw Puzzle

Jigsaw
mare   brand: 13

TORNADO'S PRINCE OF TIDES x DAKOTA SKY'S CODY TWO SOCKS

Notes:

Cody's Little Jigsaw Puzzle

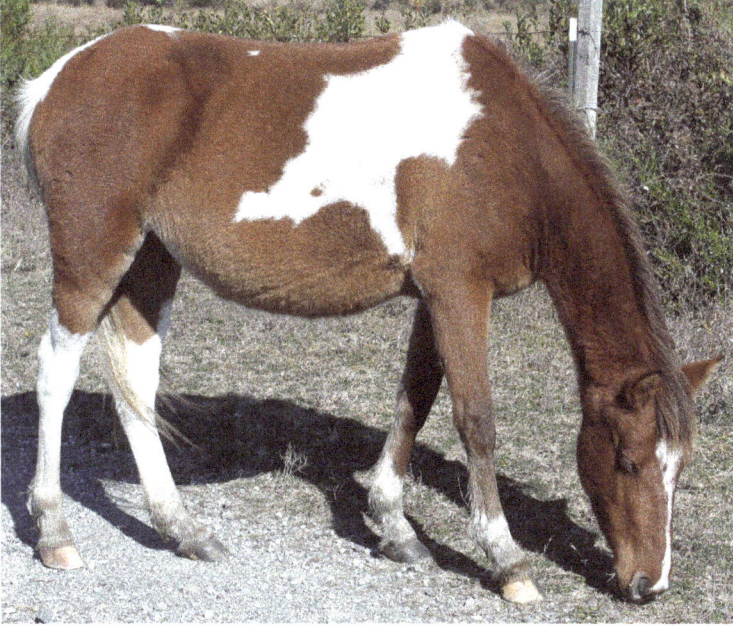

Bay Pinto

Doctor Amrien

Doc
mare   brand: 14
Wild Thing x Dakota Sky's Cody Two Socks

Notes:

_____

_____

_____

_____

_____

_____

_____

_____

_____

_____

Doctor Amrien

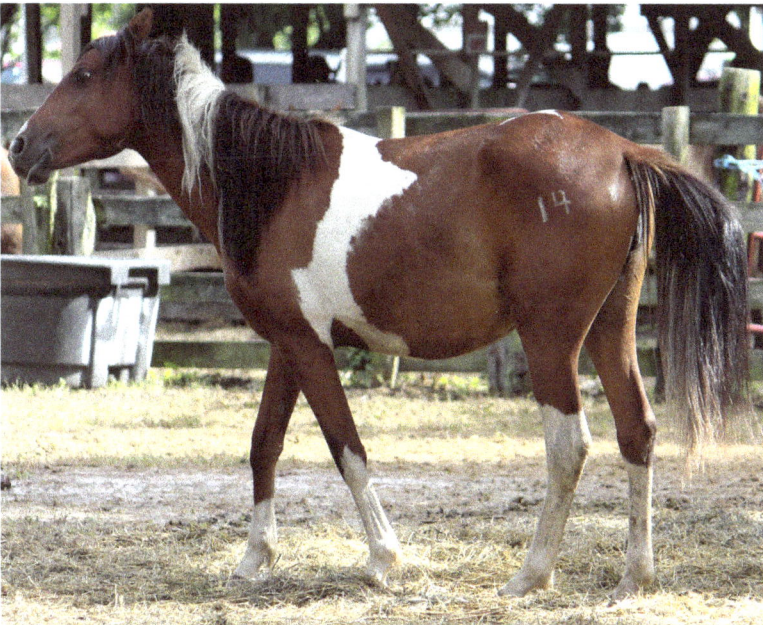

Bay Pinto

White Saddle

mare   brand: 13
WITCH DOCTOR x WILD ISLAND ORCHID

Notes:

_____

_____

_____

_____

_____

_____

_____

_____

_____

_____

_____

White Saddle

Bay Pinto

Miracle's Natural Beauty

Natural Beauty
mare　　　　　　brand: 09
MIRACLE MAN x NATURAL INNOCENCE

Notes:

_____

_____

_____

_____

_____

_____

_____

_____

_____

_____

Miracle's Natural Beauty

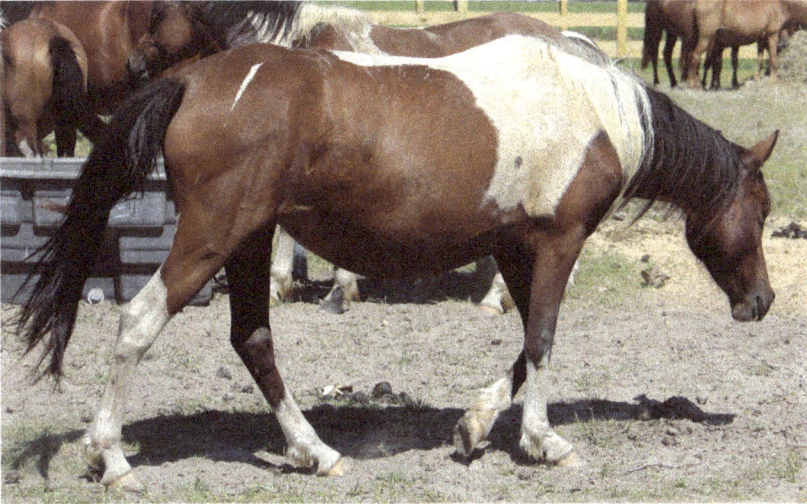

Bay Pinto

May's Grand Slam

May
mare   brand: 12

Miracle Man x Spanish Angel

Notes:

_____

_____

_____

_____

_____

_____

_____

_____

_____

_____

May's Grand Slam

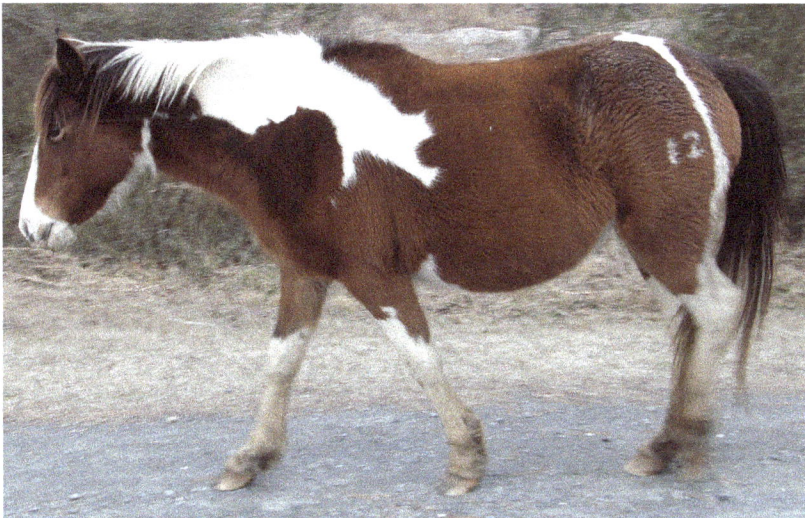

Bay Pinto

Carol's Little Freedom

Little Freedom
mare   brand: 99, partial
HURRICANE x SILK AND LACE

Notes:

_____

_____

_____

_____

_____

_____

_____

_____

_____

_____

_____

Carol's Little Freedom

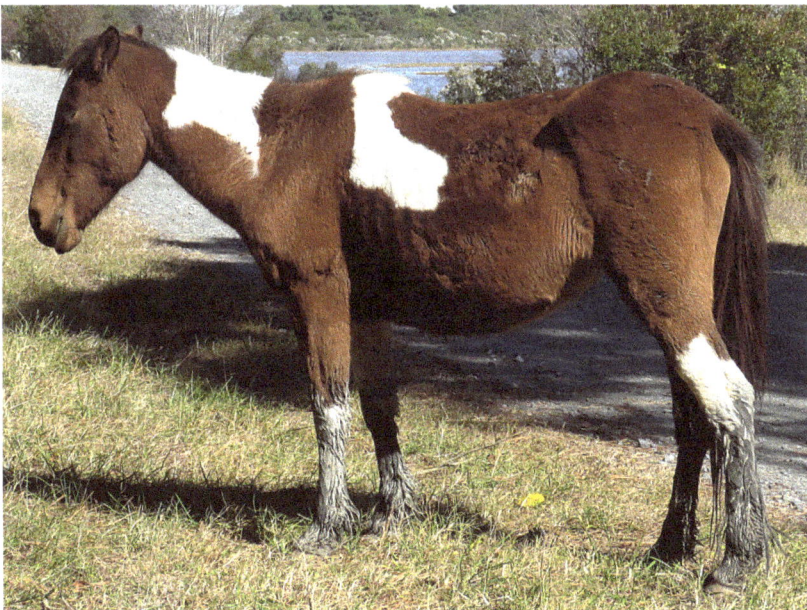

Bay Pinto

Tunie

Queenie
mare   brand: 03

WILLIE'S MAJESTIC DREAMER X SEASIDE

Notes:

_____

_____

_____

_____

_____

_____

_____

_____

_____

_____

Tunie

Bay Pinto

Wendy's Carolina Girl

Carolina Girl
mare   brand: 18
MAVERICK x ESSIE

Notes:

_____
_____
_____
_____
_____
_____
_____
_____
_____
_____
_____

Wendy's Carolina Girl

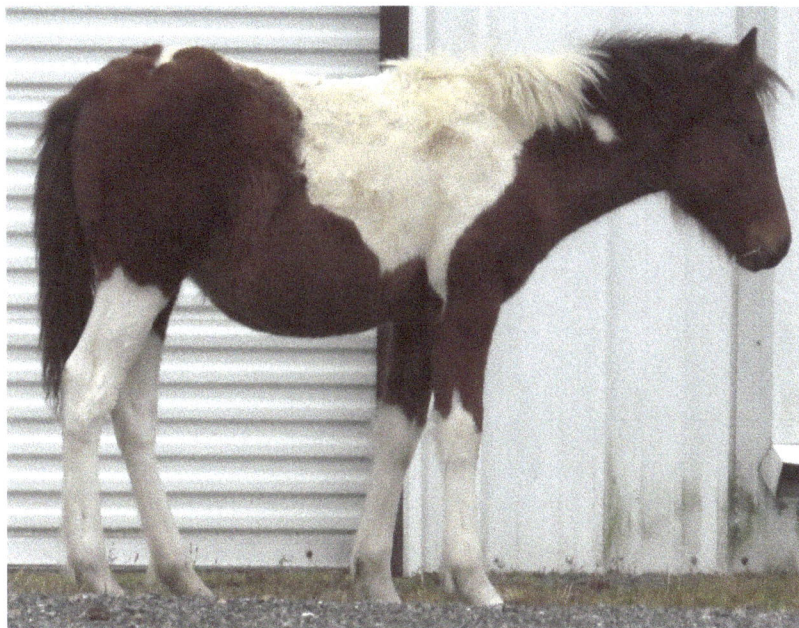

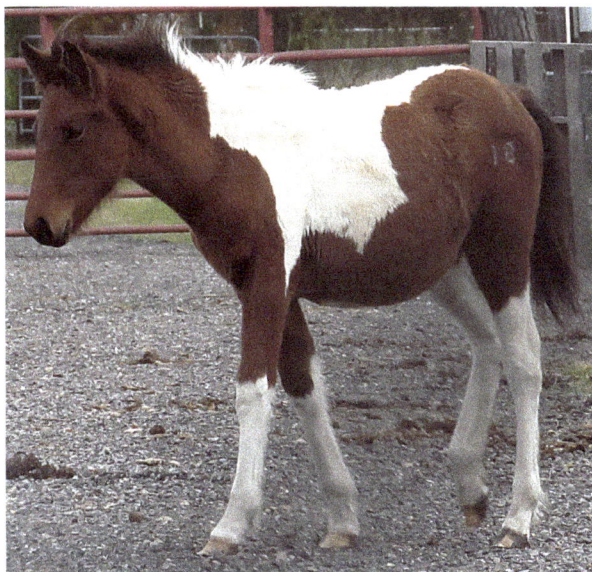

Bay Pinto

Ajax

stallion   brand: 07, partial
YANKEE SPIRIT x FOXY ASSET

Notes:

_____

_____

_____

_____

_____

_____

_____

_____

_____

_____

_____

Ajax

Bay Pinto

MissMe

mare   brand: 17
Ajax x Miracle's Natural Beauty

Notes:

_____

_____

_____

_____

_____

_____

_____

_____

_____

_____

MissMe

Bay Pinto

Babe

mare   brand: 94, partial

WITCH DOCTOR x WILD FIRE

Notes:

_____

_____

_____

_____

_____

_____

_____

_____

_____

Babe

Bay Pinto

Millennium Midnight

Oreo
mare   brand: none
MIRACLE MAN x CHANTILLY LACE

Notes:

_____

_____

_____

_____

_____

_____

_____

_____

_____

_____

Millennium Midnight

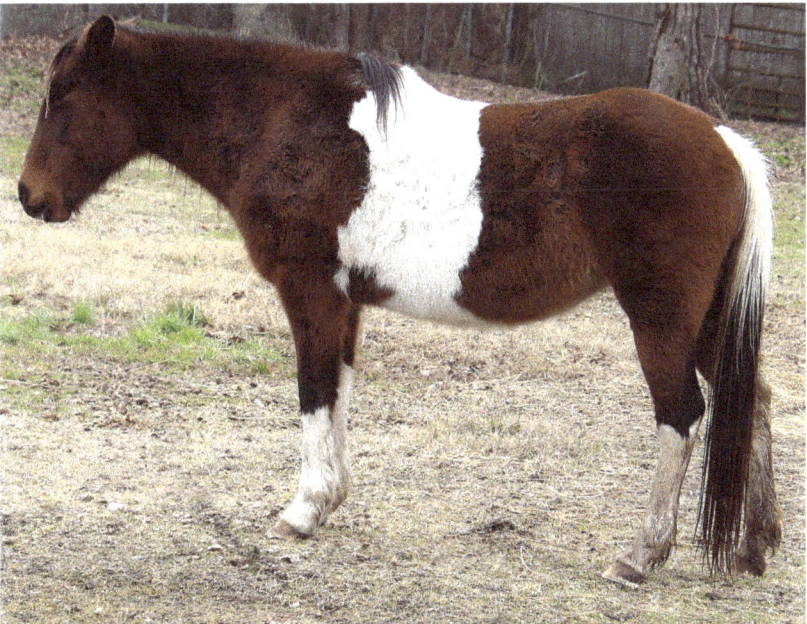

Bay Pinto

Rainbow Warrior

Napolean
stallion   brand: none

(UNKNOWN) X (UNKNOWN)

Notes:

_____

_____

_____

_____

_____

_____

_____

_____

_____

_____

Rainbow Warrior

Bay Pinto

Destiny Feathering Spirit

Destiny
mare   brand: none
Courtney's Boy x Vixen

Notes:

_____

_____

_____

_____

_____

_____

_____

_____

_____

_____

_____

Destiny Feathering Spirit

Bay Pinto

Sweetheart

mare   brand: unreadable
Wild Bill x Scotty ET

Notes:

_____
_____
_____
_____
_____
_____
_____

_____
_____
_____
_____

Sweetheart

Bay Pinto

Henry's Hidalgo

stallion   brand: 17
WILD THING X THETIS

Notes:

_____

_____

_____

_____

_____

_____

_____

_____

_____

_____

Henry's Hidalgo

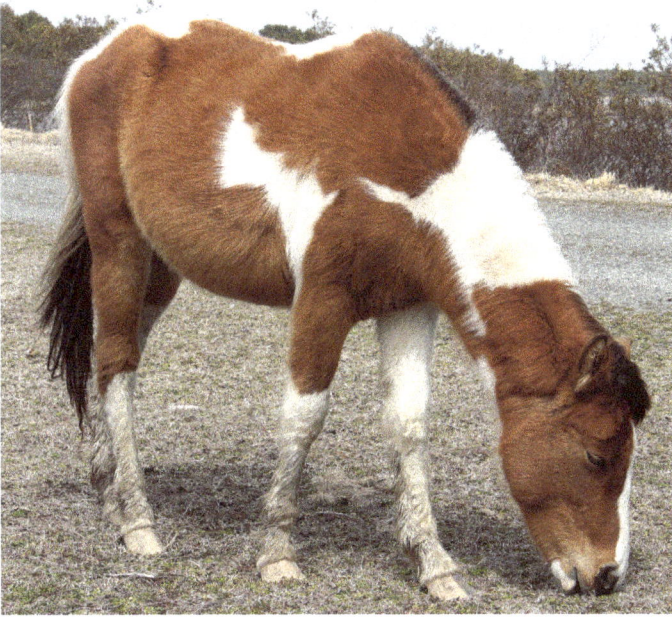

Bay Pinto

Splash

Danny's Girl
mare   brand: 14
WILD THING x SUMMER BREEZE

Notes:

_____

_____

_____

_____

_____

_____

_____

_____

_____

_____

Splash

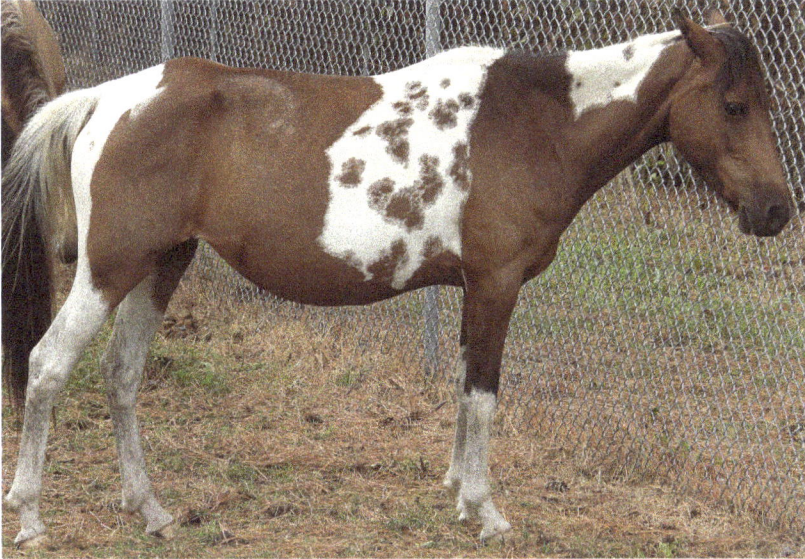

Bay Pinto

Grandma's Dream

mare   brand: 13
WILD THING x GALADRIEL

Notes:

_____

_____

_____

_____

_____

_____

_____

_____

_____

_____

Grandma's Dream

Bay Pinto

Loveland's Secret Feather

Secret, Feather
mare   brand: 12
WILD THING x GALADRIEL

Notes:

_____

_____

_____

_____

_____

_____

_____

_____

_____

_____

_____

Loveland's Secret Feather

Bay Pinto

Wild Thing

stallion   brand: none
HURRICANE x JUST MY STYLE

Notes:

_____

_____

_____

_____

_____

_____

_____

_____

_____

_____

Wild Thing

Bay Pinto

Chickadee

mare   brand: 13
Courtney's Boy x Black Star

Notes:

_____

_____

_____

_____

_____

_____

_____

_____

_____

_____

Chickadee

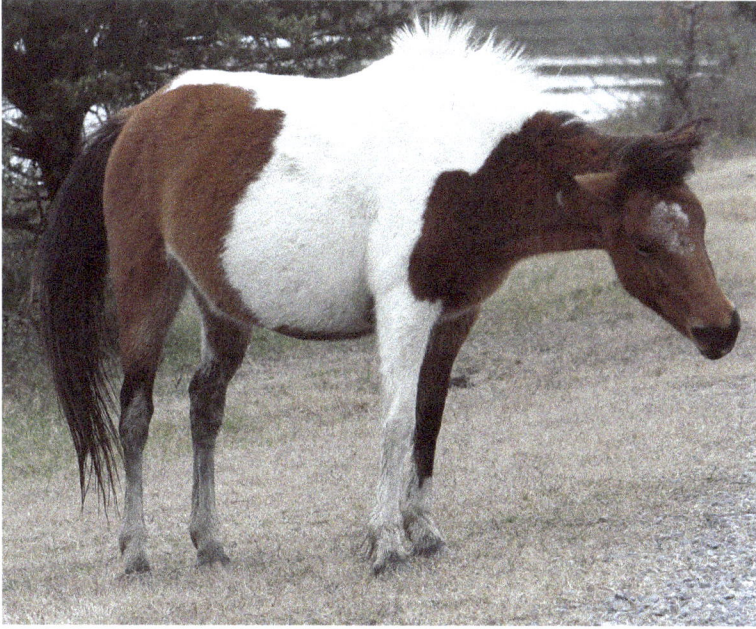

Bay Pinto

Wildest Dreams

mare   brand: 08
MIRACLE MAN x NATURAL INNOCENCE

Notes:

_____

_____

_____

_____

_____

_____

_____

_____

_____

_____

_____

Wildest Dreams

Bay Pinto

Black Star

mare   brand: none
WITCH DOCTOR x RAP THE WIND

Notes:

_____

_____

_____

_____

_____

_____

_____

_____

_____

_____

Black Star

Bay Pinto

Marguerite of Chincoteague

mare   brand: 13
ARCHER'S GAMBIT x MIRACLE'S NATURAL BEAUTY

Notes:

Marguerite of Chincoteague

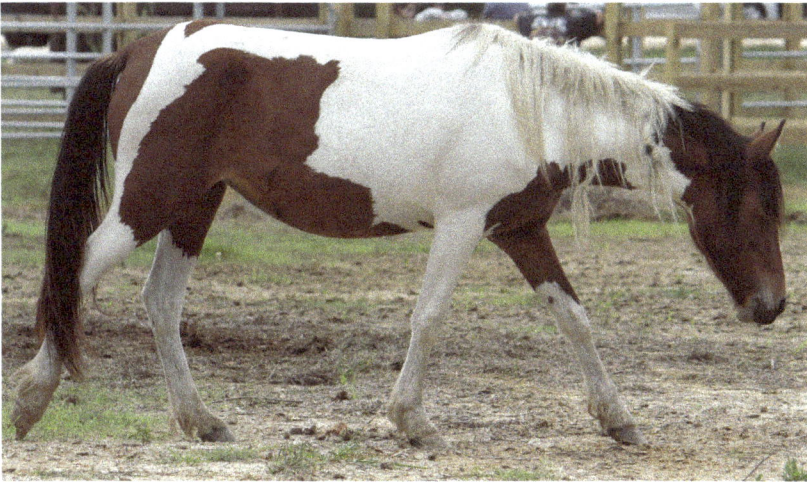

Bay Pinto

Shy Anne

Half n Half
mare   brand: none
HOT AIR BALLOON x SUNSHINE

Notes:

_____

_____

_____

_____

_____

_____

_____

_____

_____

_____

Shy Anne

Bay Pinto

Fifteen Friends of Freckles

Freckles
mare   brand: 06
NORTH STAR x MARK'S ISLAND LIBERTY

Notes:

Fifteen Friends of Freckles

Bay Pinto

Skylark

mare   brand: none
WILD THING x FOXY ASSET

Notes:

_____

_____

_____

_____

_____

_____

_____

_____

_____

_____

_____

Skylark

Bay Pinto

Scotty ET

ET
mare   brand: 02, partial
Attitude x Black Star

Notes:

_____

_____

_____

_____

_____

_____

_____

_____

_____

_____

Scotty ET

Bay Pinto

Winter Moon

Moon
mare   brand: none
(UNKNOWN) X (UNKNOWN)

Notes:

_____

_____

_____

_____

_____

_____

_____

Winter Moon

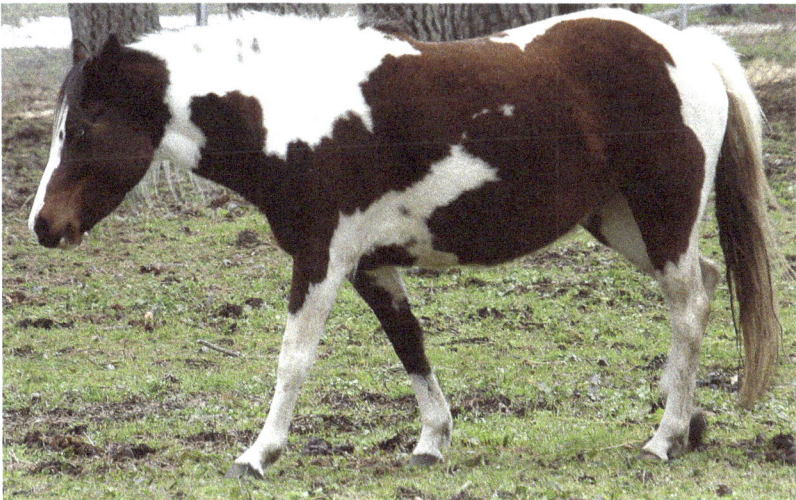

Bay Pinto

Summer

mare   brand: none
WH Nightwind x (unknown)

Notes:

_____

_____

_____

_____

_____

_____

_____

_____

_____

_____

Summer

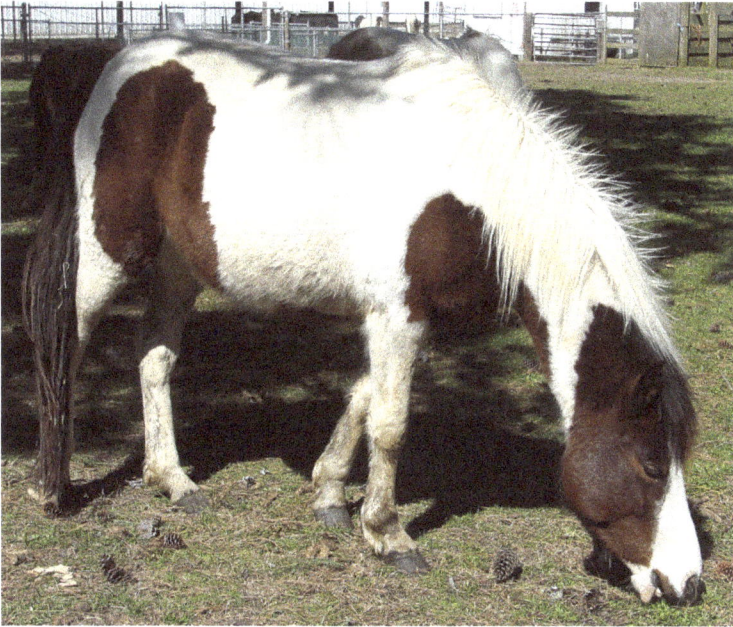

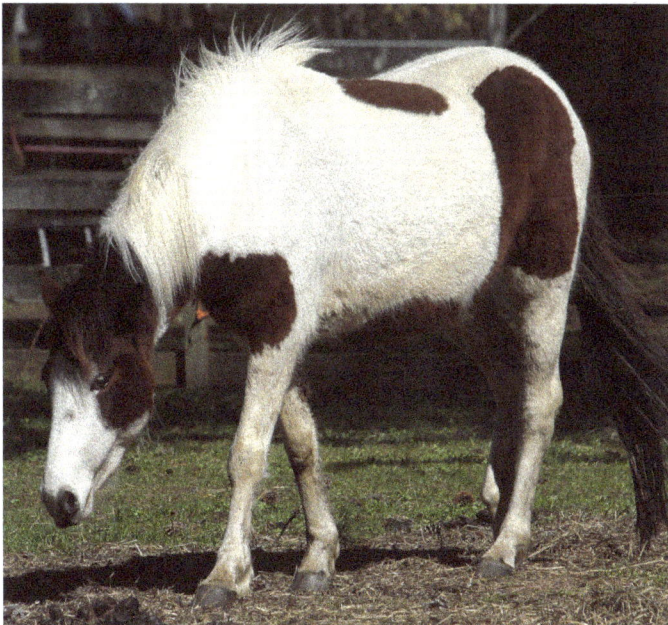

Bay Pinto

Seaside Miracle

mare　　　　　　brand: F
MIRACLE MAN x SEASIDE

Notes:

_____

_____

_____

_____

_____

_____

_____

_____

_____

_____

Seaside Miracle

Bay Pinto

A Splash of Freckles

Splash of Freckles
mare   brand: unreadable
Leonard Stud x Fifteen Friends of Freckles

Notes:

_____

_____

_____

_____

_____

_____

_____

_____

_____

_____

A Splash of Freckles

Bay Pinto

Maverick

stallion   brand: 14
WILD THING x WITCH KRAFT

Notes:

_____

_____

_____

_____

_____

_____

_____

_____

_____

_____

Maverick

Bay Pinto

Got Milk

Anna
mare   brand: none
Witch Doctor x Waterkolor

Notes:

_____

_____

_____

_____

_____

_____

_____

_____

_____

_____

_____

Got Milk

Bay Pinto

Heide's Sky

mare　　　　　　brand: none
Ken x Fifteen Friends of Freckles

Notes:

_____

_____

_____

_____

_____

_____

_____

_____

_____

_____

_____

Heide's Sky

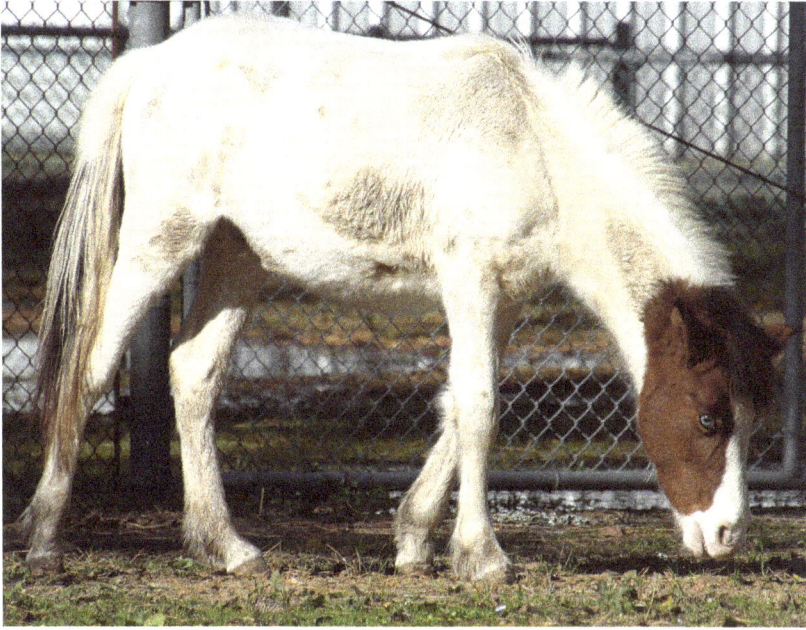

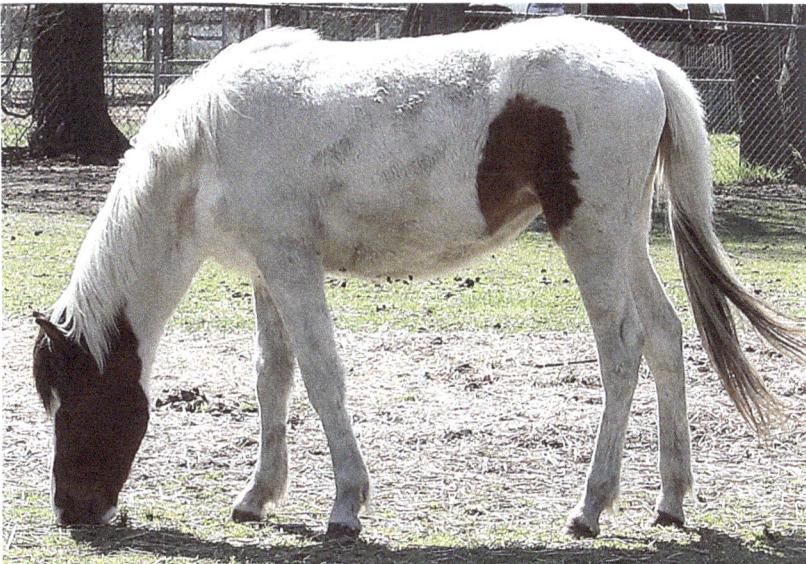

Black

CLG Ember

Ember
mare   brand: 18
Surfer's Riptide x Black Pearl

Notes:

_____
_____
_____
_____
_____
_____

_____
_____
_____
_____

CLG Ember

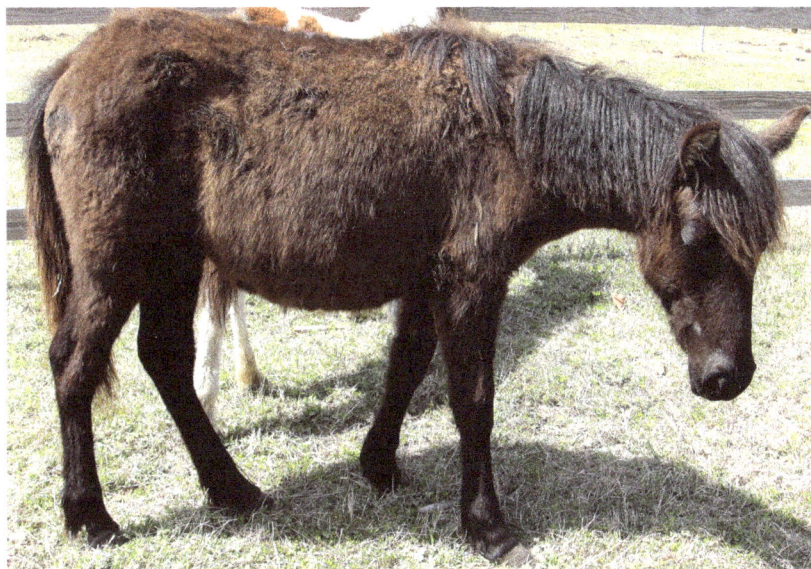

Black

Talia/Evan's Angel

Evan's Angel, Talia
mare   brand: 17
MAVERICK x SURFIN' CHANTEL

Notes:

_____

_____

_____

_____

_____

_____

_____

_____

_____

_____

_____

_____

Talia/Evan's Angel

Black

Milly Sue

mare   brand: 17
Surfer's Riptide x Leah's Bayside Angel

Notes:

Milly Sue

CLG Surfer's Blue Moon

Blue, Blue Moon, Surfer's Blue Moon
mare   brand: 15
SURFER DUDE x GOT MILK

Notes:

CLG Surfer's Blue Moon

Black Comparision Chart

Name	Pg #	Brand	Mane	Face
Ace's Black Tie Affair	120	07	right	
CLG Ember	110	18	right	
CLG Surfer's Blue Moon	116	15	even	baldface
Milly Sue	114	17	right	
Talia/Evan's Angel	112	17	right	

NOTES

Ace's Black Tie Affair is included here even though he is technically a pinto. His markings are so minimal that he is routinely wrongly identified as solid black.

Left & right refers to the animal's left & right.

Mane: left = falls to the left **right** = falls to the right **split** = significant portion falls on left and right

Legs				Notable Details
R F	**R B**	**L F**	**L B**	**Notable Details**
sock	stocking	sock	stocking	stallion; small upside heart behind left front leg; very long forelock
sock	sock	sock	sock	blue eyes
sock		sock	sock	7 in brand easily mistaken for 1

R F = right front   **R B** = right back **L F** = left front   **L B** = left back
sock = white well below the knee   **stocking** = white near and above the knee

baldface = white covers most of the face   **blaze** = white streak running down the length of the face   **snip** = white spot on the muzzle   **star** = white spot on the forehead

Black Pinto

Ace's Black Tie Affair

Ace
stallion   brand: 07
Centaur x Susie Q

Notes:

_____

_____

_____

_____

_____

_____

_____

_____

_____

Ace's Black Tie Affair

Black Pinto

Poco's Starry Night

Starry Night, Cash
mare   brand: 12
LEONARD STUD x POCO LATTE PW

Notes:

_____

_____

_____

_____

_____

_____

Poco's Starry Night

Black Pinto

Pixie Dust

mare   brand: 14

A<small>CE'S</small> B<small>LACK</small> T<small>IE</small> A<small>FFAIR</small> x A<small>NGEL</small> W<small>INGS</small>

Notes:

_____

_____

_____

_____

_____

_____

_____

_____

_____

Pixie Dust

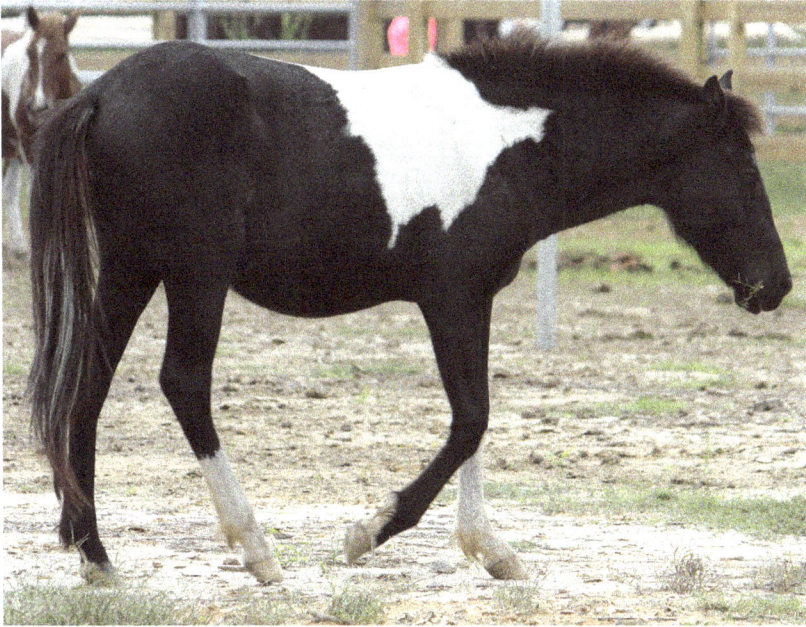

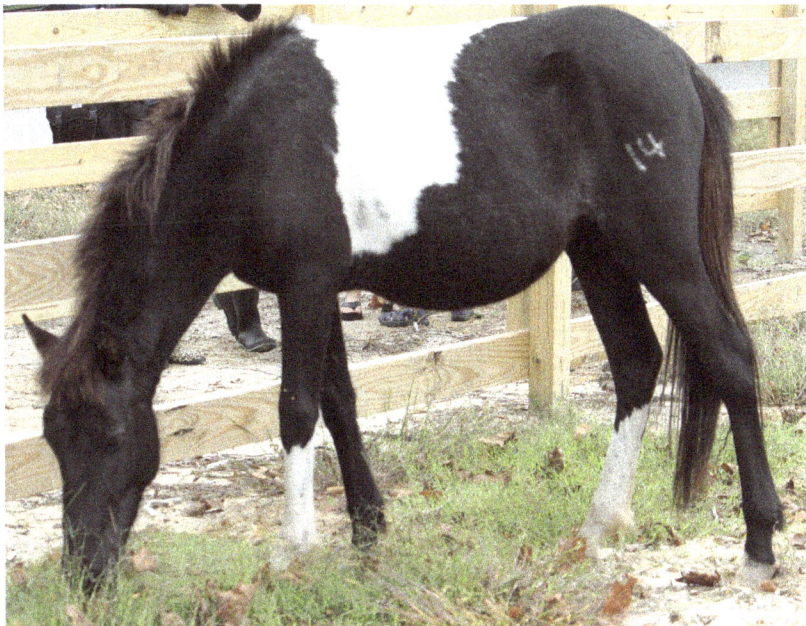

Black Pinto

Gracey

mare   brand: 13
Sockett To Me x Leah's Bayside Angel

Notes:

_____

_____

_____

_____

_____

_____

_____

_____

_____

_____

Gracey

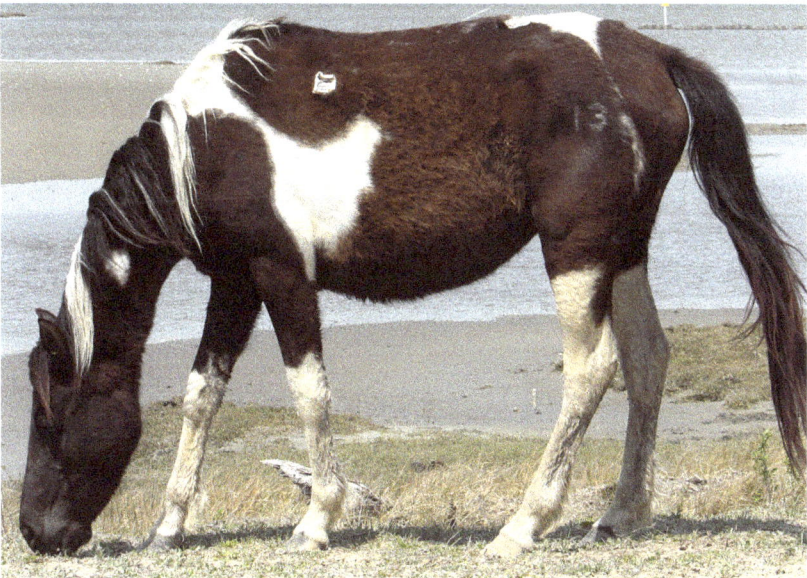

Black Pinto

Black Pearl

Pearl
mare   brand: 14
Sockett To Me x Leah's Bayside Angel

Notes:

_____

_____

_____

_____

_____

_____

_____

_____

_____

Black Pearl

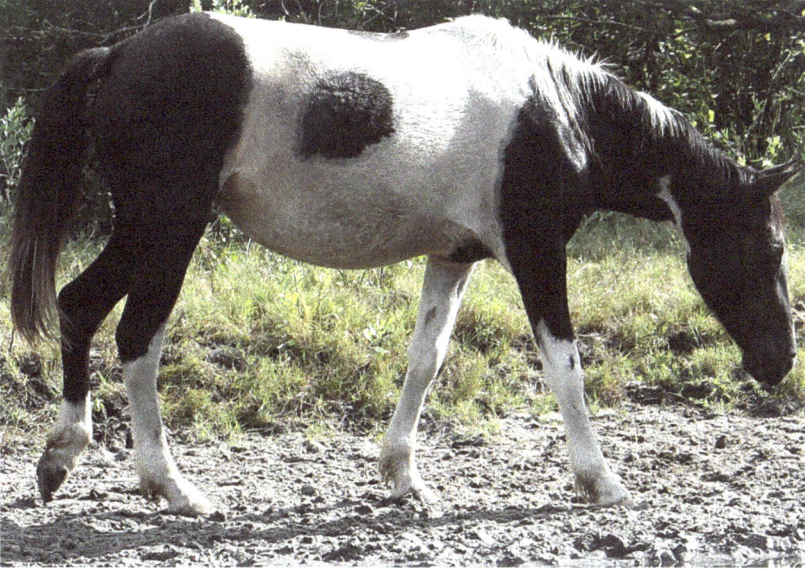

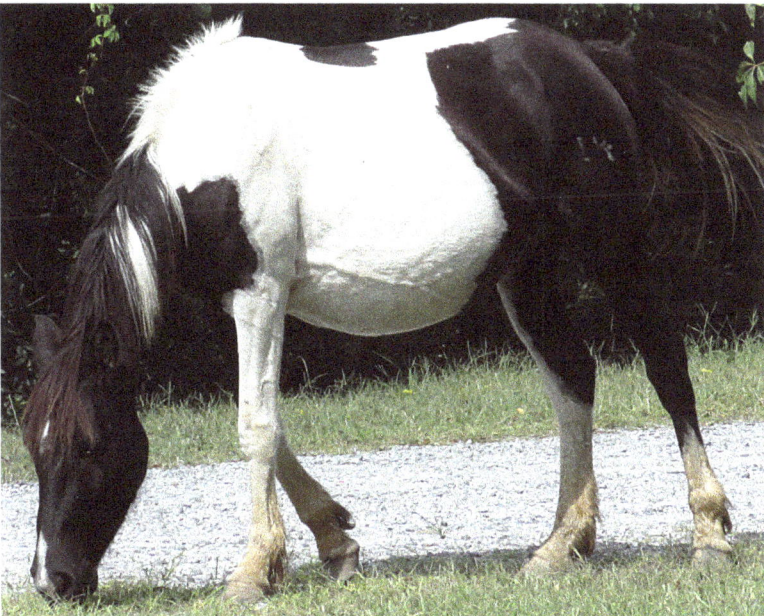

Black Pinto

Baybe

Baby
mare   brand: none
TUFFER THAN LEATHER x APRIL MOON

Notes:

_____

_____

_____

_____

_____

_____

_____

_____

_____

_____

Baybe

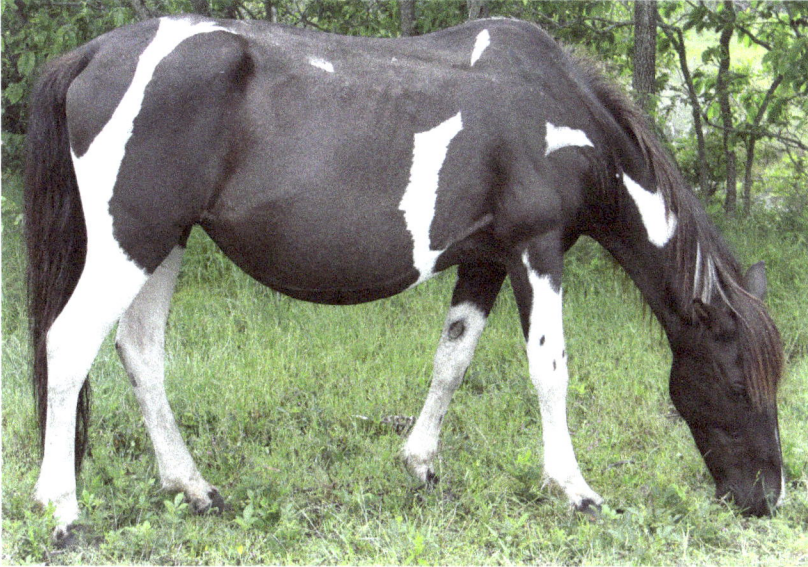

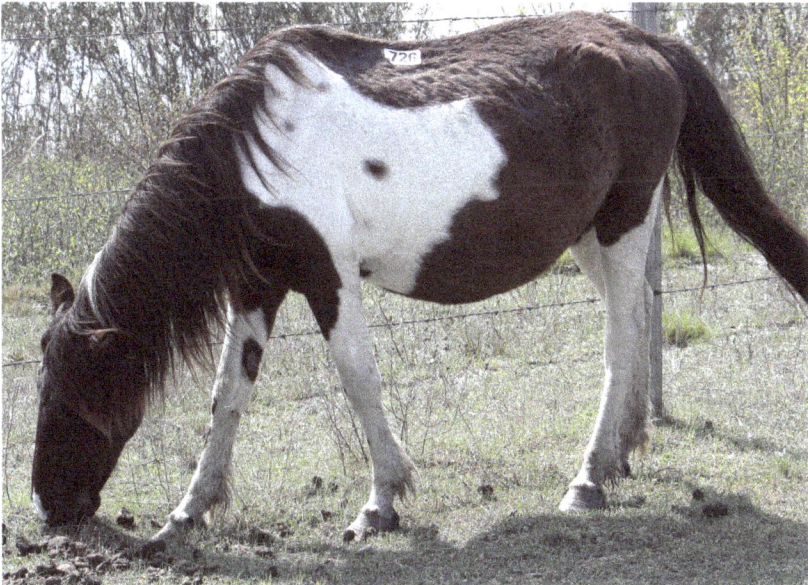

Black Pinto

Calendar Girl

mare   brand: 17
WH Nightwind x (unknown)

Notes:

_____

_____

_____

_____

_____

_____

_____

_____

_____

_____

_____

Calendar Girl

Black Pinto

Beach Boy

Saltwater Renegade, Renegade
stallion   brand: 15
WH Nightwind x WH Sea Breeze

Notes:

_____

_____

_____

_____

_____

_____

_____

_____

_____

_____

Beach Boy

Buckskin

Alice's Sandcastle

mare   brand: 12
NORTH STAR x LIVING LEGEND

Notes:

_____

_____

_____

_____

_____

_____

_____

_____

_____

_____

Alice's Sandcastle

Buckskin

Ivana Marie Zustan

Zustan
mare   brand: 16
Little Dolphin x Jessica's Sea Star Sandy

Notes:

Ivana Marie Zustan

Buckskin

Jessica's Sea Star Sandy

Jessica's Sandy
mare   brand: 06
TORNADO x PHILLY GIRL

Notes:

_____

_____

_____

_____

_____

_____

_____

_____

_____

_____

_____

Jessica's Sea Star Sandy

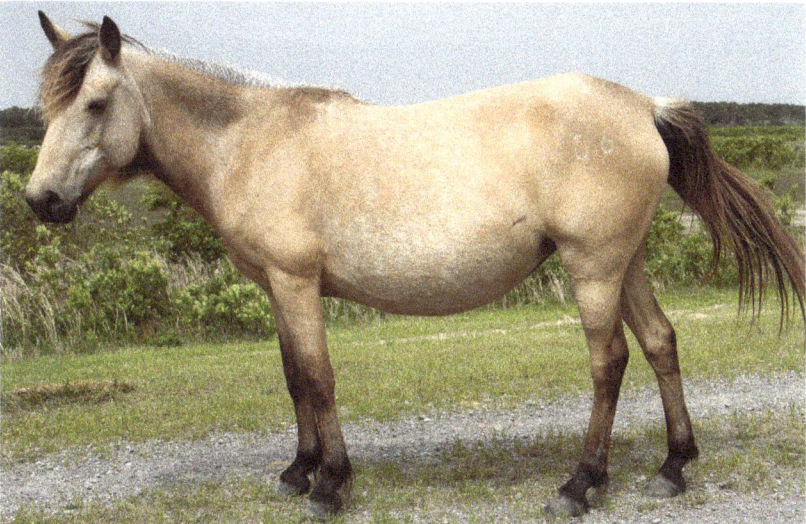

Buckskin

Landrie's Georgia Peach

Georgia Peach
mare   brand: 04
TORNADO x PHILLY GIRL

Notes:

_____

_____

_____

_____

_____

_____

_____

_____

_____

_____

_____

Landrie's Georgia Peach

Buckskin

Liz's Serenity

mare   brand: 17
WILD BILL x LANDRIE'S GEORGIA PEACH

Notes:

_____

_____

_____

_____

_____

_____

_____

_____

_____

_____

Liz's Serenity

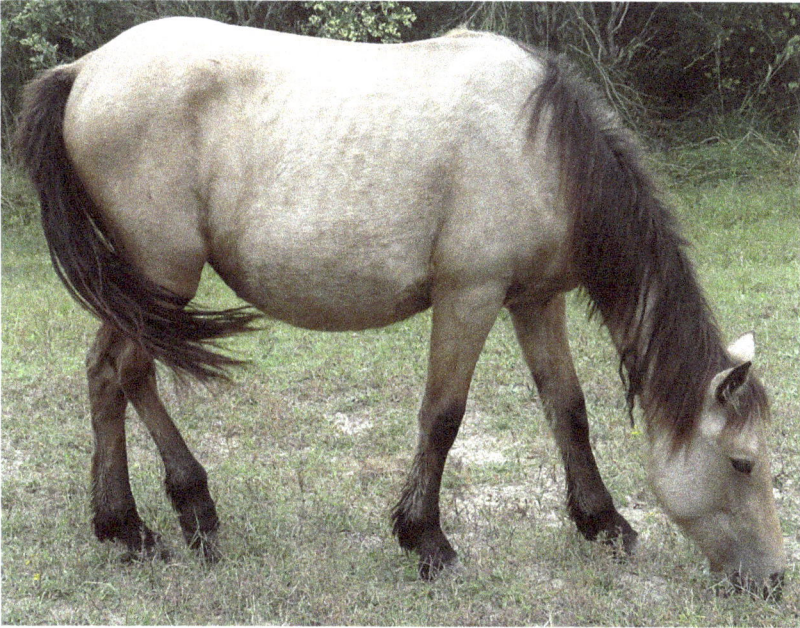

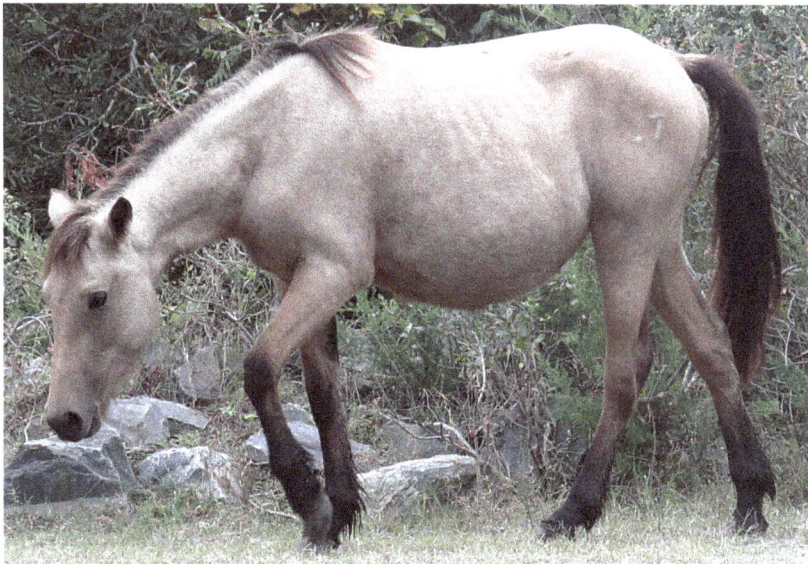

Buckskin

Poco Latte PW

mare   brand: 02
Gunner's Moon x Misty Dawn

Notes:

_____

_____

_____

_____

_____

_____

_____

_____

_____

Poco Latte PW

Buckskin

Sunrise Ocean Tides

Sunny
mare   brand: 15
LITTLE DOLPHIN x JESSICA'S SEA STAR SANDY

Notes:

_____

_____

_____

_____

_____

_____

_____

_____

_____

_____

_____

Sunrise Ocean Tides

Buckskin

Too Grand

Salt Water Taffee
mare   brand: 00
Cinnamon Hologram x Merry Teapot's High Bid

Notes:

_____

_____

_____

_____

_____

_____

_____

_____

_____

_____

_____

Too Grand

Kachina Grand Star

Kachina
mare   brand: 05, partial
NORTH STAR x TOO GRAND

Notes:

_____

_____

_____

_____

_____

_____

_____

_____

_____

_____

_____

Kachina Grand Star

Buckskin Comparison Chart

Name	Pg #	Brand	Mane	Face
Alice's Sandcastle	136	12	right	
Ivana Marie Zustan	138	16	right	
Jessica's Sea Star Sandy	140	06	right	
Kachina Grand Star	152	05, partial	left	star
Landrie's Georgia Peach	142	04	left	
Liz's Serenity	144	17	right	
Poco Latte PW	146	02	right	
Sunrise Ocean Tides	148	15	right	
Too Grand	150	00	left	

NOTES

Left & right refers to the animal's left & right.

Mane: left = falls to the left **right** = falls to the right **split** = significant portion falls on left and right

Buckskin Comparison Chart

Legs				Notable Details
R F	R B	L F	L B	
				forelock hangs to eyes
	sock		sock	forelock hangs to eyes
				dark dappled coat; forelock hangs to eyes
	sock			forelock hangs to eyes

R F = right front   R B = right back L F = left front   L B = left back
sock = white well below the knee   stocking = white near and above the knee

baldface = white covers most of the face   blaze = white streak running down the length of the face   snip = white spot on the muzzle   star = white spot on the forehead

155

Buckskin Pinto

Molly's Rosebud

Rosie
mare   brand: none

Yankee Spirit x Merry Teapot's High Bid

Notes:

_____

_____

_____

_____

_____

_____

_____

_____

_____

_____

Molly's Rosebud

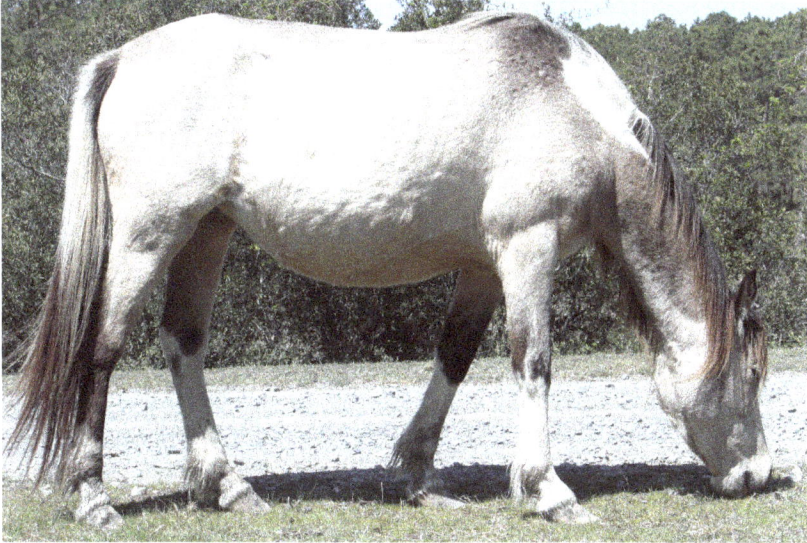

Buckskin Pinto

CLG Bay Princess

Bay Princess
mare   brand: 16
Tornado's Prince of Tides x Baybe

Notes:

_____

_____

_____

_____

_____

_____

_____

_____

_____

_____

CLG Bay Princess

Buckskin Pinto

Badabing

mare   brand: 15
TORNADO'S PRINCE OF TIDES X ELLA OF ASSATEAGUE

Notes:

_____

_____

_____

_____

_____

_____

_____

_____

_____

Badabing

Buckskin Pinto

CLG ToMorrow's Tidewater Twist

Twist, Triple T, Tidewater Twist
stallion   brand: 17
TORNADO'S LEGACY x SWEETHEART

Notes:

CLG ToMorrow's Tidewater Twist

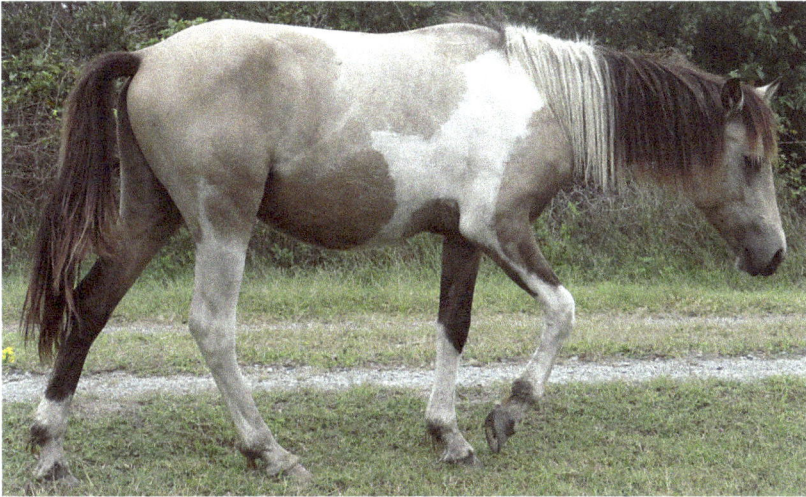

Buckskin Pinto

Tornado's Legacy

Legacy, Lil Tornado
stallion   brand: 07
Tornado x Unci

Notes:

_____

_____

_____

_____

_____

_____

_____

_____

_____

_____

_____

Tornado's Legacy

Buckskin Pinto

Randy

mare   brand: 14
Tornado's Prince of Tides x Baybe

Notes:

_____

_____

_____

_____

_____

_____

_____

_____

_____

_____

Randy

Buckskin Pinto

Serendipity

mare   brand: 18

Maverick x Calcetín

Notes:

_____

_____

_____

_____

_____

_____

_____

_____

_____

_____

_____

Serendipity

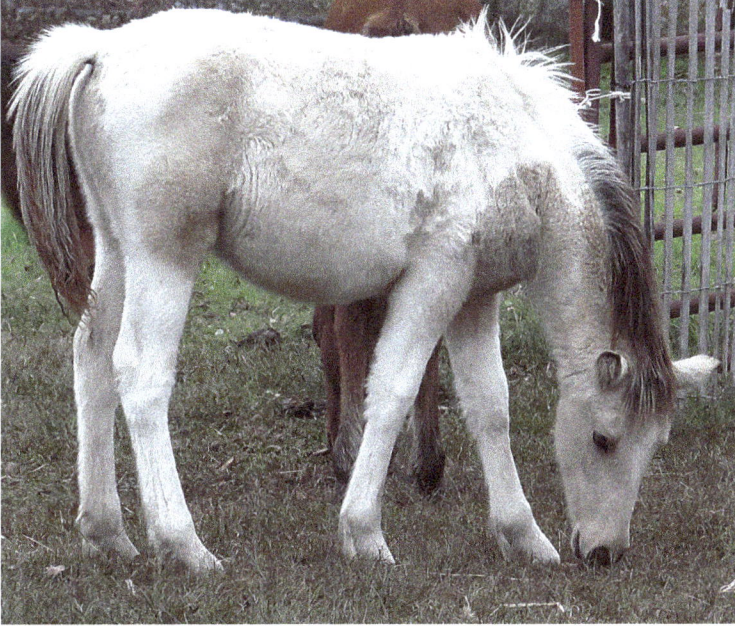

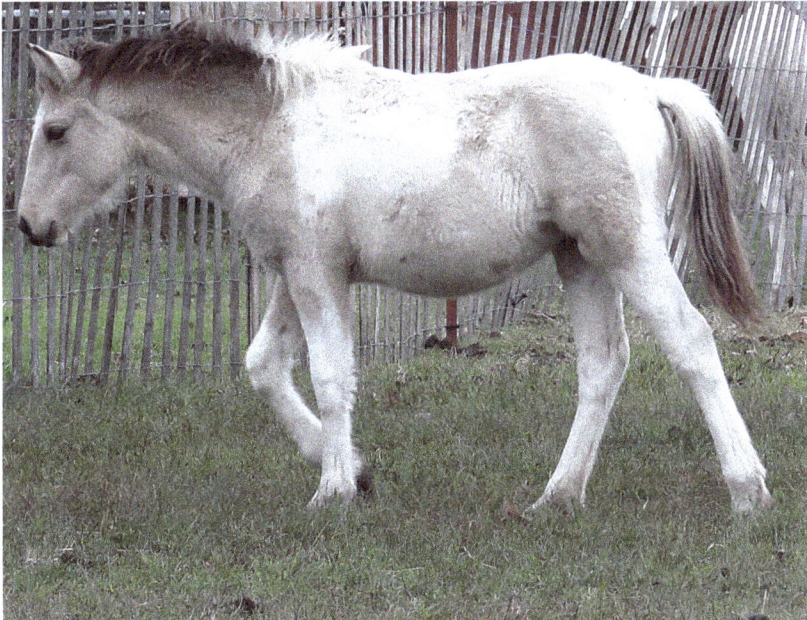

Buckskin Pinto

Tidewater Treasure

Treasure
mare   brand: none
CHEROKEE CHIEF x BLONDE

Notes:

_____
_____
_____
_____
_____
_____
_____

_____
_____
_____
_____

Tidewater Treasure

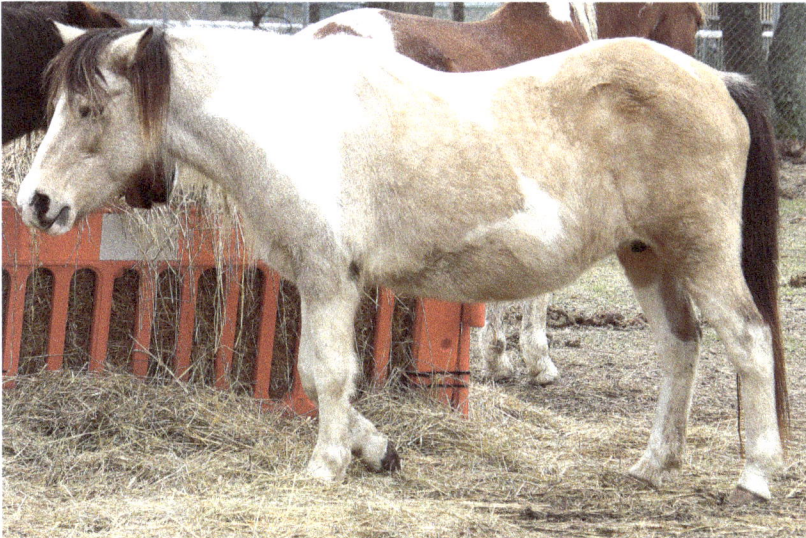

Chestnut

JABATAA

mare   brand: 02
CHEROKEE CHIEF x ROSIE O' GRADY

Notes:

_____

_____

_____

_____

_____

_____

_____

_____

_____

_____

JABATAA

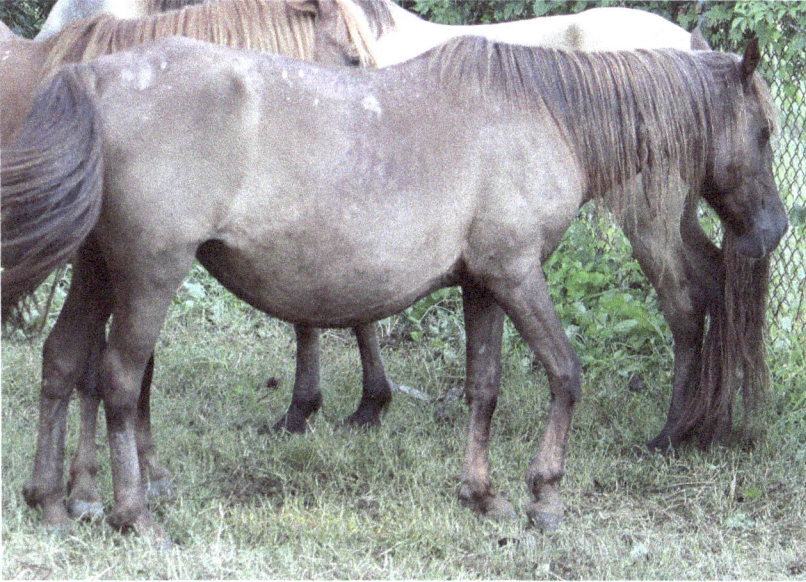

Chestnut

Surfer's Shining Star

Gingersnap
mare   brand: 15
SURFER DUDE x TSG's ELUSIVE STAR

Notes:

_____

_____

_____

_____

_____

_____

_____

_____

_____

_____

Surfer's Shining Star

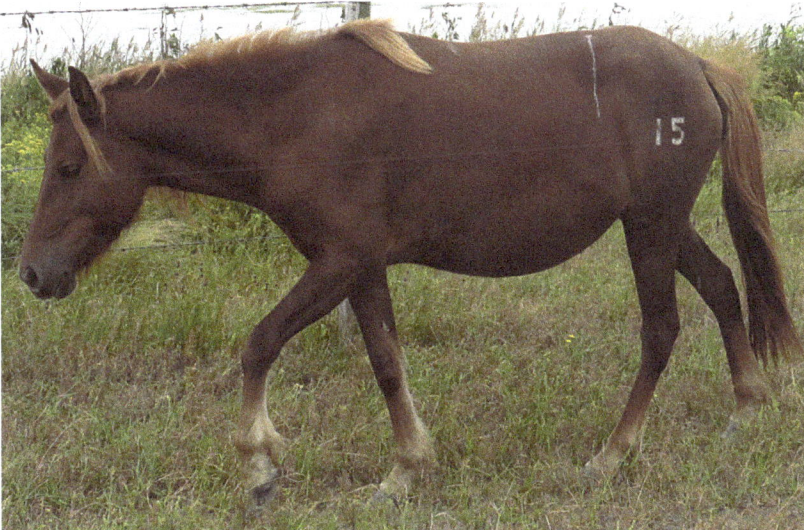

Chestnut

Surfin' Chantel

mare   brand: 13
RAINBOW WARRIOR x SURFIN' SCARLET

Notes:

_____
_____
_____
_____
_____
_____
_____

_____
_____
_____
_____

Surfin' Chantel

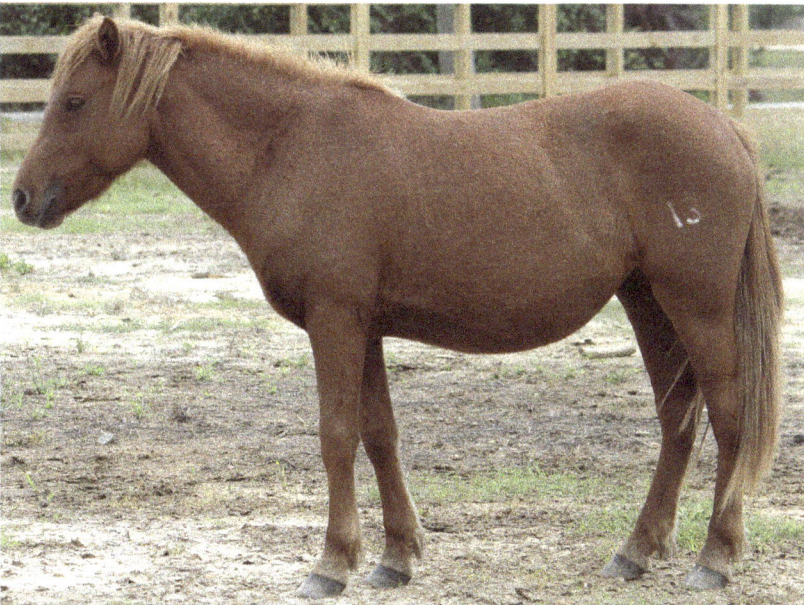

Chestnut

Susana

mare   brand: 01

CHEROKEE CHIEF x GLAMOUR GIRL

Notes:

Susana

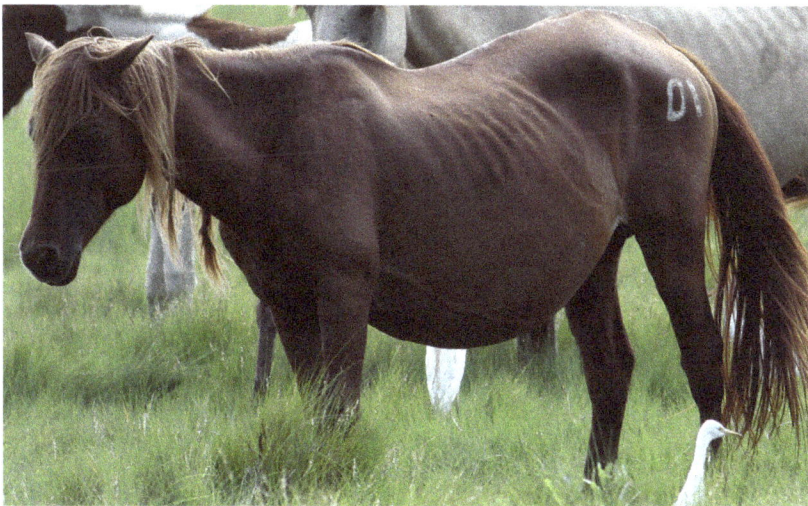

Chestnut

Suzy's Sweetheart

mare   brand: 98
CHEROKEE CHIEF x VOYAGER

Notes:

_____

_____

_____

_____

_____

_____

_____

_____

_____

_____

_____

Suzy's Sweetheart

Chestnut

Tuleta Star

mare   brand: 02
CHEROKEE CHIEF x A TOUCH OF DUST

Notes:

_____

_____

_____

_____

_____

_____

_____

_____

_____

_____

Tuleta Star

Chestnut

Cinnamon Blaze

mare   brand: unreadable
(UNKNOWN) X SNEAKERS

Notes:

_____

_____

_____

_____

_____

_____

_____

_____

_____

_____

Cinnamon Blaze

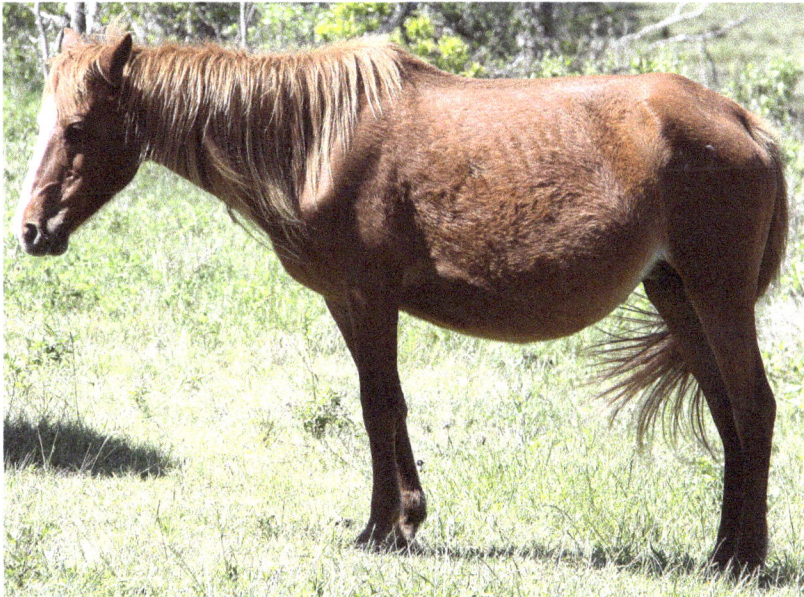

Chestnut

Kimmee-Sue

mare   brand: 12
Courtney's Boy x Cinnamon Blaze

Notes:

_____

_____

_____

_____

_____

_____

_____

_____

_____

_____

Kimmee-Sue

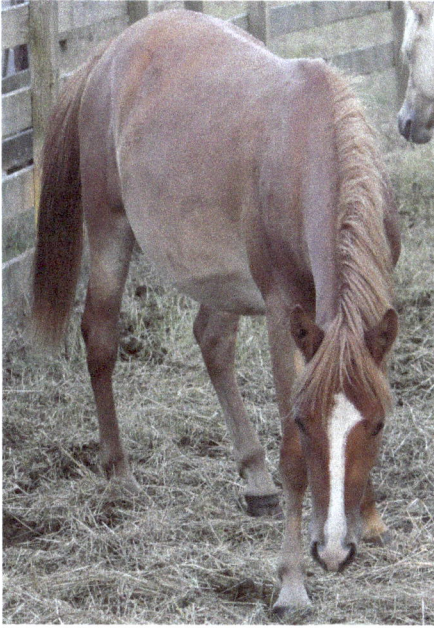

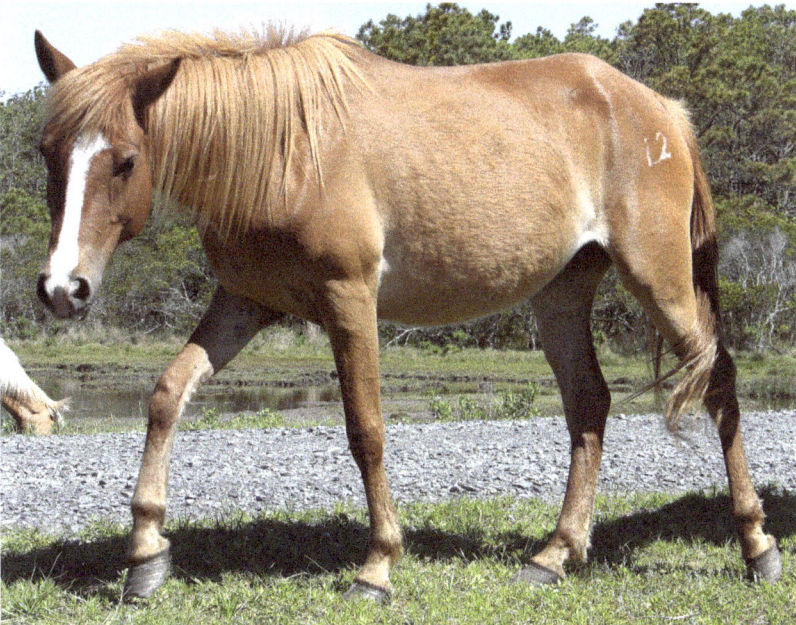

Chestnut

Surfin' Scarlet

Scarlet
mare   brand: 00
SURFER DUDE x SURF QUEEN

Notes:

_____

_____

_____

_____

_____

_____

_____

_____

_____

Surfin' Scarlet

Chestnut

Precious Jewel

mare   brand: 14
PHANTOM MIST x UNCI

Notes:

_____

_____

_____

_____

_____

_____

_____

_____

_____

_____

Precious Jewel

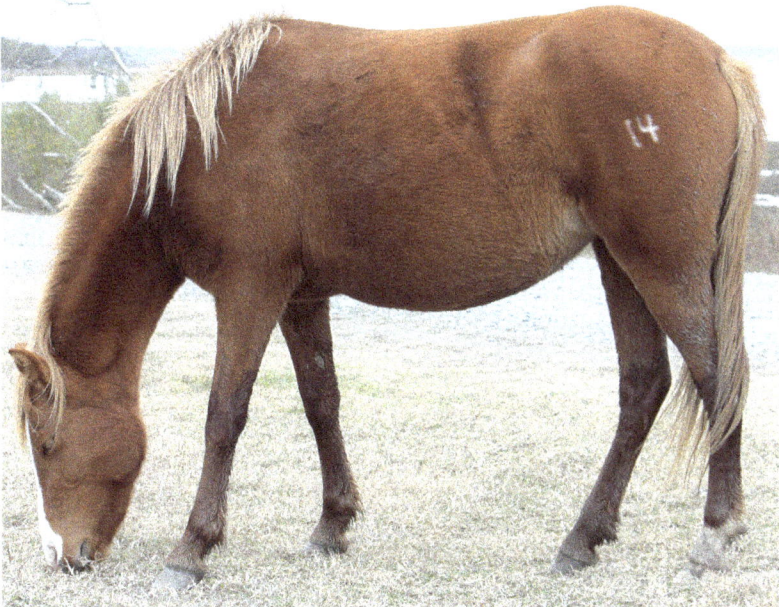

Chestnut

Unforgettable 2001

Diamond
mare   brand: none
Hurricane x Just My Style

Notes:

_____

_____

_____

_____

_____

_____

_____

_____

_____

_____

_____

Unforgettable 2001

Chestnut

Judy's Little Smooch

Smooch
mare   brand: none
SURFER'S RIPTIDE x BUTTERFLY KISSES

Notes:

_____

_____

_____

_____

_____

_____

_____

_____

_____

_____

Judy's Little Smooch

Chestnut

Surfer Dude's Gidget

Gidget
mare   brand: F, 02, partial
SURFER DUDE x VIRGINIA BELLE

Notes:

Surfer Dude's Gidget

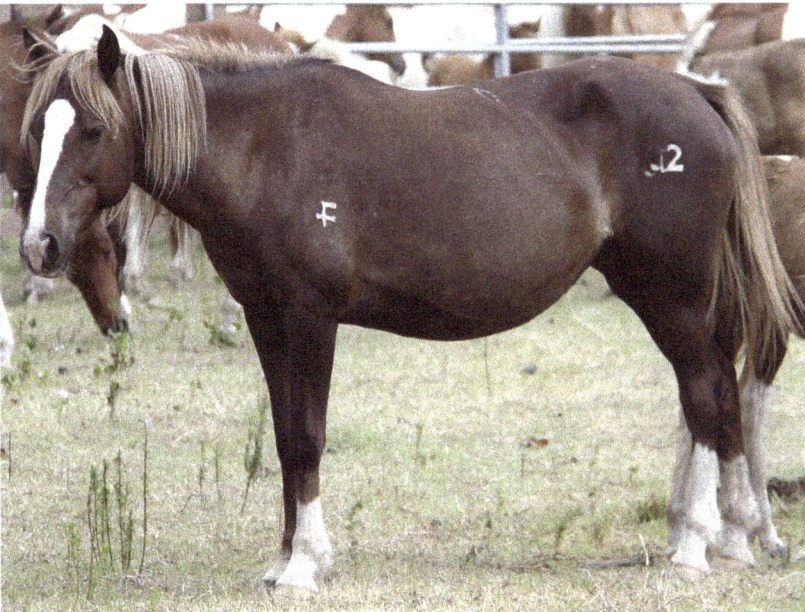

Chestnut

Dreamer's Gift

mare   brand: 12

Surfer Dude x Lyra's Vega

Notes:

_____

_____

_____

_____

_____

_____

_____

_____

_____

_____

Dreamer's Gift

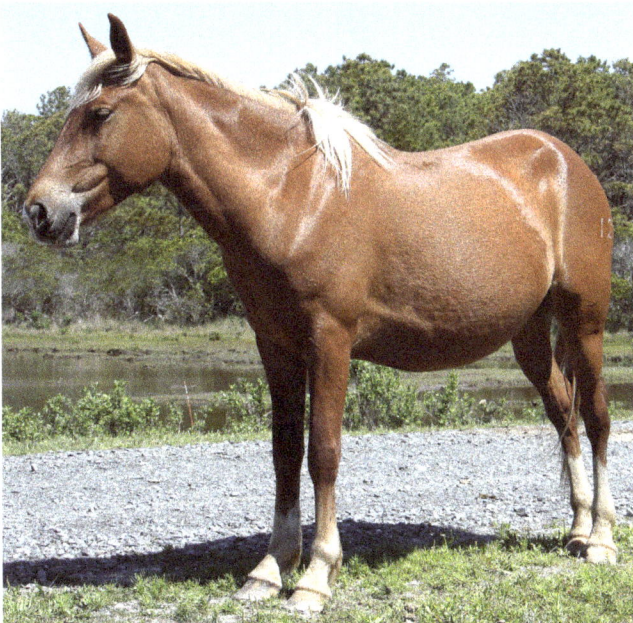

Chestnut

Surfer Princess

mare   brand: 15
SURFER DUDE x SURF QUEEN

Notes:

_____

_____

_____

_____

_____

_____

_____

_____

_____

_____

Surfer Princess

Chestnut

Surfette

mare   brand: 17
(UNKNOWN) X SUNDANCE

Notes:

_____
_____
_____
_____
_____
_____
_____

_____
_____
_____

Surfette

Chestnut

Ken

Valentine
stallion   brand: 08
WILD THING x STAR GAZER

Notes:

_____

_____

_____

_____

_____

_____

_____

_____

_____

_____

Ken

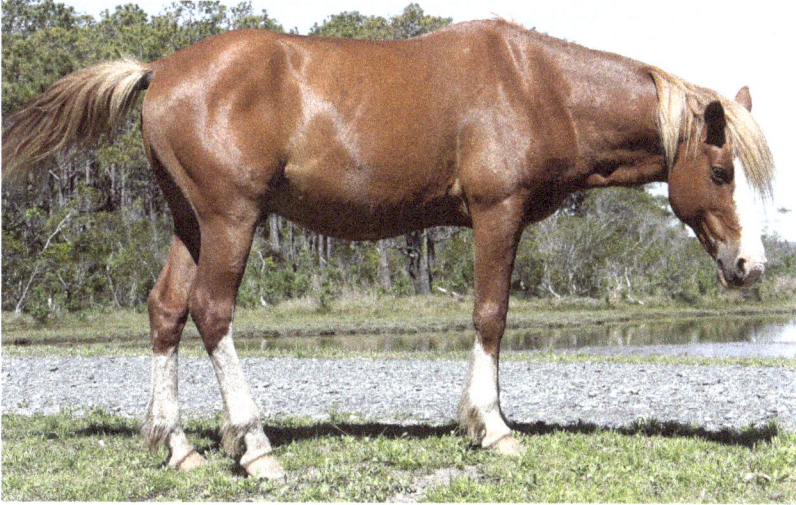

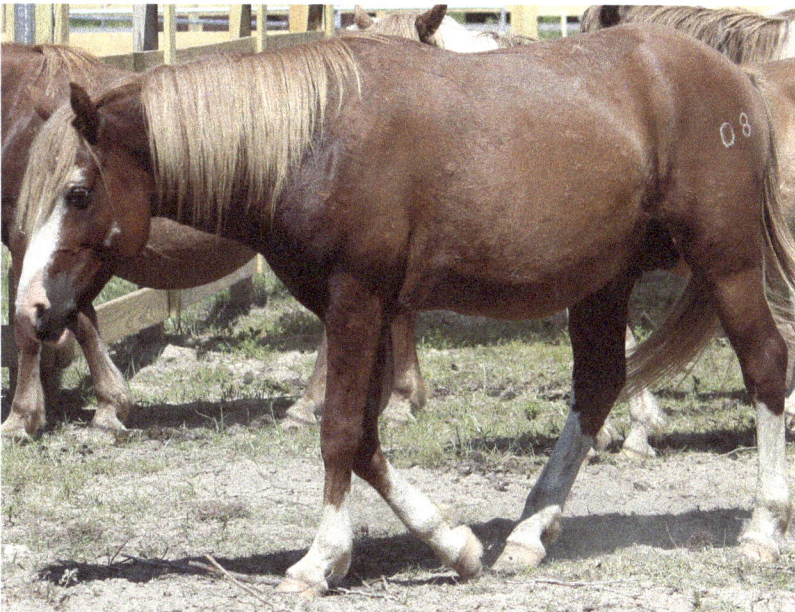

Chestnut

Dreamer's Stardust

Stardust
mare   brand: 18
KEN x DREAMER'S GIFT

Notes:

_____

_____

_____

_____

_____

_____

_____

_____

_____

Dreamer's Stardust

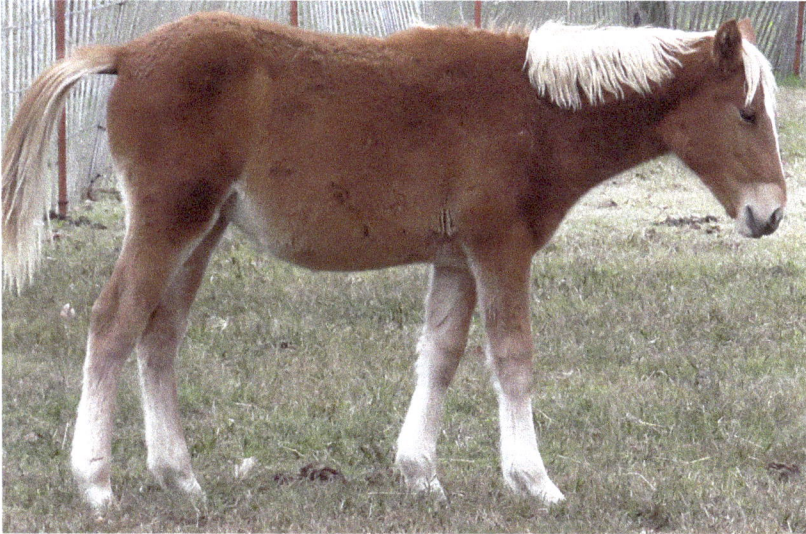

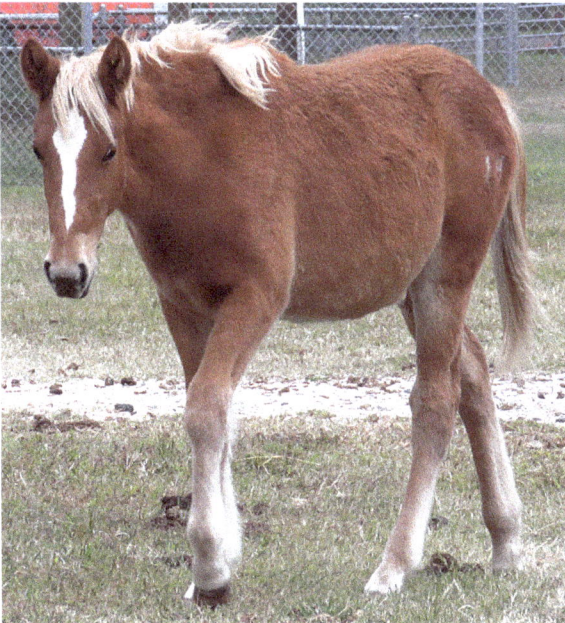

Chestnut

Surfer's Riptide

Riptide
stallion   brand: 09, partial

Surfer Dude x Surf Queen

Notes:

_____

_____

_____

_____

_____

_____

_____

_____

_____

_____

Surfer's Riptide

Chestnut Comparison Chart

Name	Pg #	Brand	Mane	Face
Cinnamon Blaze	184	unreadable	left	blaze
Dreamer's Gift	198	12	split	star and snip
Dreamer's Stardust	206	18	split	blaze
JABATAA	172	02	right	
Judy's Little Smooch	194		right	blaze
Ken	204	08	left	baldface
Kimmee-Sue	186	12	left	blaze
Precious Jewel	190	14	split	blaze
Surfer Dude's Gidget	196	F, 02, partial	split	blaze
Surfer Princess	200	15	right	star and snip
Surfer's Riptide	208	09, partial	right	baldface
Surfer's Shining Star	174	15	right	
Surfette	202	17	right	blaze
Surfin' Chantel	176	13	right	
Surfin' Scarlet	188	00	right	star
Susana	178	01	right	
Suzy's Sweetheart	180	98	right	
Tuleta Star	182	02	right	star and snip
Unforgettable 2001	192		left	star

NOTES

Left & right refers to the animal's left & right.

Mane: left = falls to the left **right** = falls to the right **split** = significant portion falls on left and right

Chestnut Comparison Chart

Legs				Notable Details
R F	R B	L F	L B	
sock	sock	sock	sock	blond mane & tail
stocking	stocking	stocking	stocking	blond mane & tail
				very dark coat
	stocking			
sock	stocking	sock	stocking	stallion; small white kiss mark on left cheek; blond mane & tail
			sock	
	sock	sock	sock	dark coat; much lighter mane & tail
sock	sock	sock	sock	
stocking	stocking	stocking	stocking	stallion; dark coat; blond mane & tail; long forelock covers eyes
				dark red coat; mane & tail a little lighter
sock	sock	sock	sock	dark brown
				small whitish diamond-shaped patch on right hip; long forelock
				forelock hangs to eyes
				small stature; long forelock
				long forelock
		sock	sock	dark coat

R F = right front   R B = right back L F = left front   L B = left back
sock = white well below the knee   stocking = white near and above the knee

baldface = white covers most of the face   blaze = white streak running down the length of the face   snip = white spot on the muzzle   star = white spot on the forehead

211

Chestnut Pinto

Catwalk's Olympic Glory

Glory
mare   brand: 16

Aᴊᴀx x Cᴀᴛᴡᴀʟᴋ Cʜᴀᴏs

Notes:

_____

_____

_____

_____

_____

_____

_____

_____

_____

_____

Catwalk's Olympic Glory

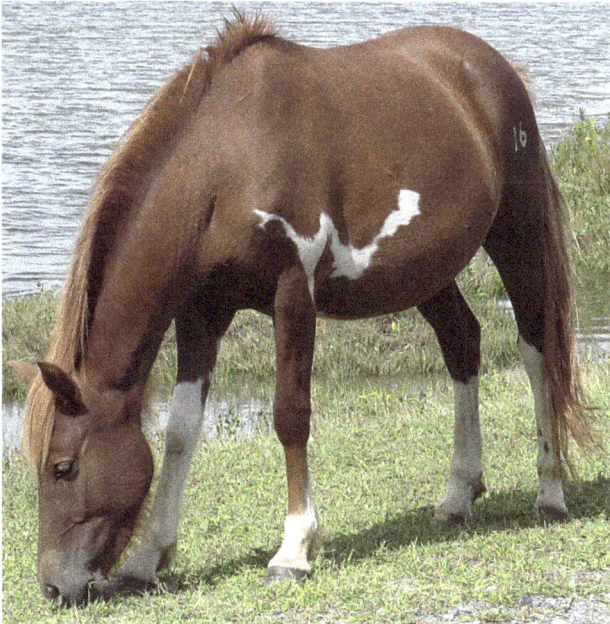

Chestnut Pinto

Chili

Lil Miss Hot Stuff
mare   brand: 17, partial
CHIEF GOLDEN EAGLE X CLOUDBURST

Notes:

Chili

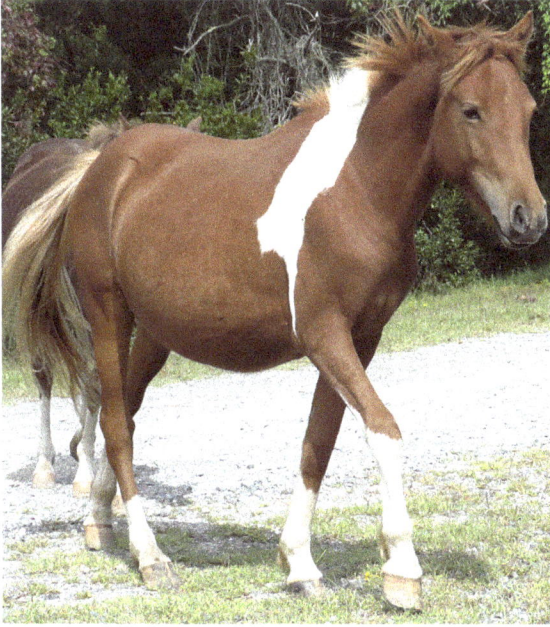

Chestnut Pinto

Slash of White

mare   brand: 98
WITCH DOCTOR x SWEET MISCHIEF

Notes:

_____

_____

_____

_____

_____

_____

_____

_____

_____

_____

Slash of White

Chestnut Pinto

Lefty's Checkmark

Butterfly
mare   brand: none
CHEROKEE CHIEF x RAPT IN PAINT

Notes:

_____

_____

_____

_____

_____

_____

_____

_____

_____

Lefty's Checkmark

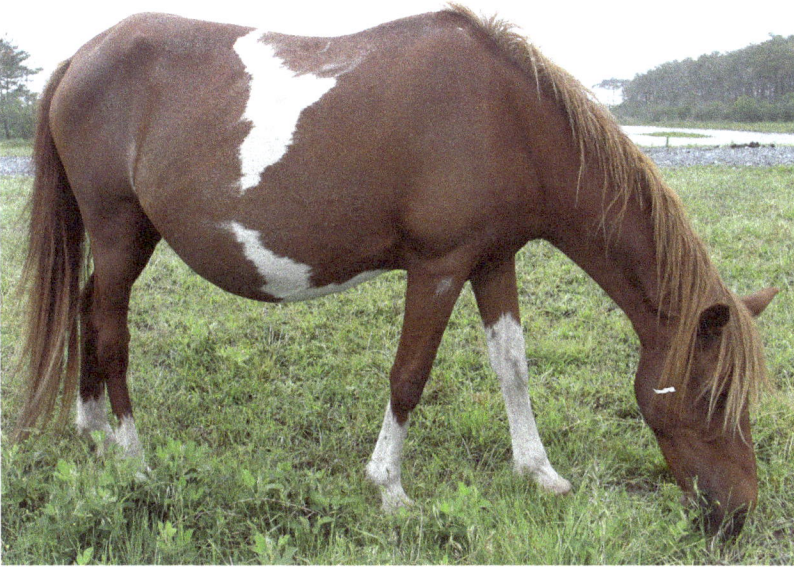

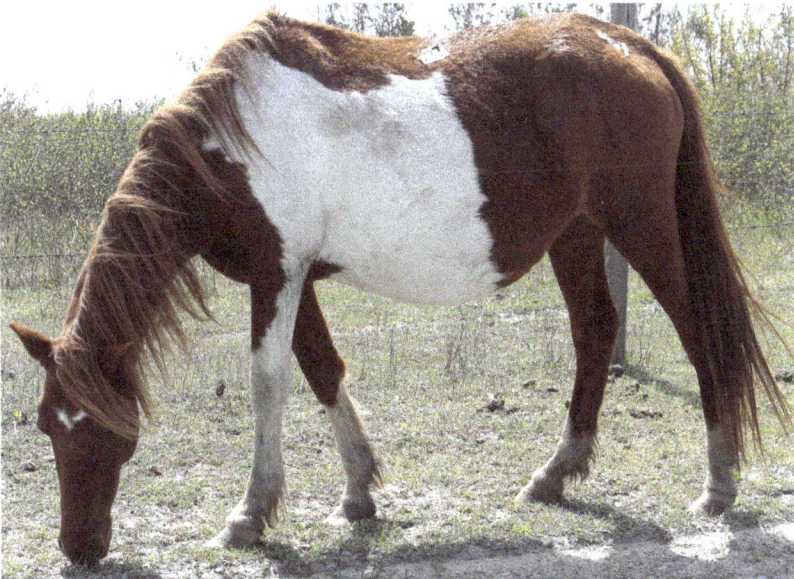

Chestnut Pinto

CJ SAMM'N

mare   brand: 06

NORTH STAR x SLASH OF WHITE

Notes:

_____

_____

_____

_____

_____

_____

_____

_____

_____

_____

CJ SAMM'N

Chestnut Pinto

Kimball's Rainbow Delight

Rainy, Rainbow Delight
mare   brand: 06, partial
NORTH STAR x RAMBLING RUBY

Notes:

Kimball's Rainbow Delight

Chestnut Pinto

Good Ole Days Bailey's Star

Star
mare   brand: none
(UNKNOWN) x (UNKNOWN)

Notes:

_____

_____

_____

_____

_____

_____

_____

_____

_____

_____

Good Ole Days Bailey's Star

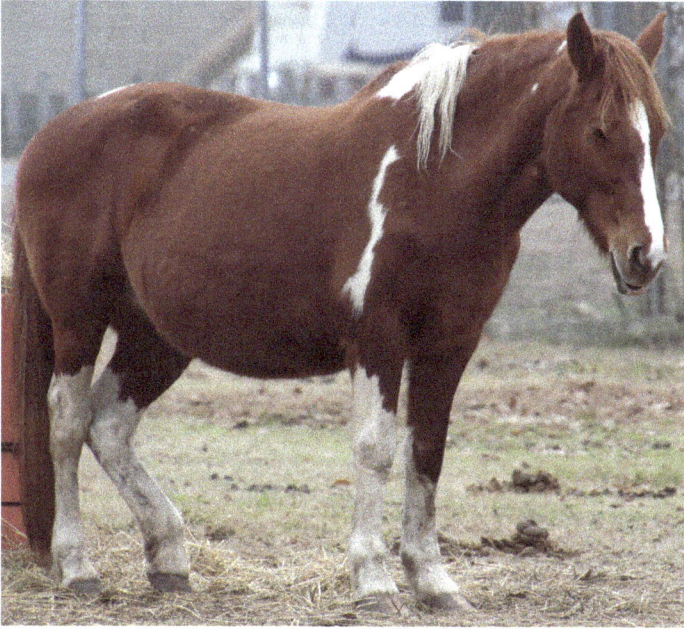

Chestnut Pinto

Tiger Lily

Waterbaby
mare   brand: none
CHEROKEE CHIEF x VOYAGER

Notes:

_____

_____

_____

_____

_____

_____

_____

_____

_____

_____

Tiger Lily

Chestnut Pinto

Pony Girl's Bliss

mare   brand: 17
Effie's Papa Bear x Carol's Little Freedom

Notes:

_____

_____

_____

_____

_____

_____

_____

_____

_____

_____

Pony Girl's Bliss

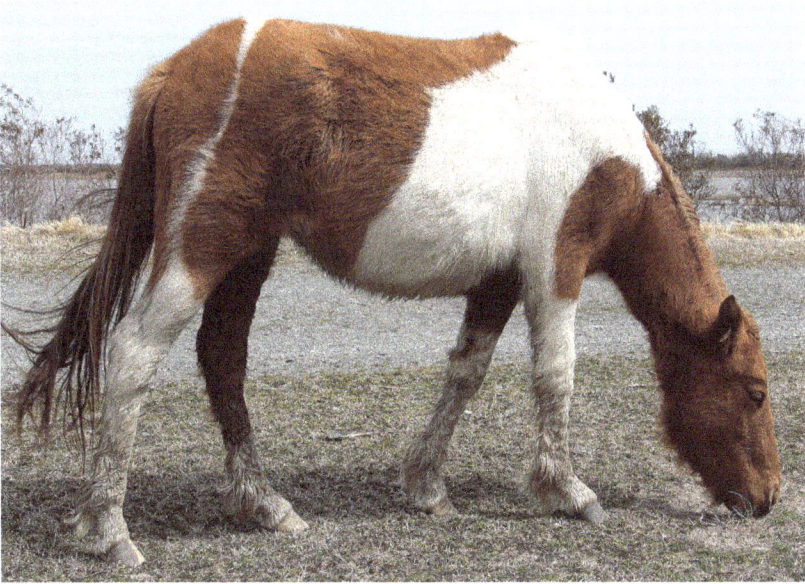

Chestnut Pinto

Susie Q

Lady Hook
mare   brand: 96
PREMIERRE x VIXEN

Notes:

_____

_____

_____

_____

_____

_____

_____

_____

_____

_____

_____

Susie Q

Chestnut Pinto

Catwalk Chaos

Margarita
mare   brand: none
Chaos x Paint by Number

Notes:

_____

_____

_____

_____

_____

_____

_____

_____

_____

_____

_____

Catwalk Chaos

233

Chestnut Pinto

Carli Marie

mare   brand: 18
Ace's Black Tie Affair x Gidget's Beach Baby

Notes:

_____

_____

_____

_____

_____

_____

_____

_____

_____

_____

Carli Marie

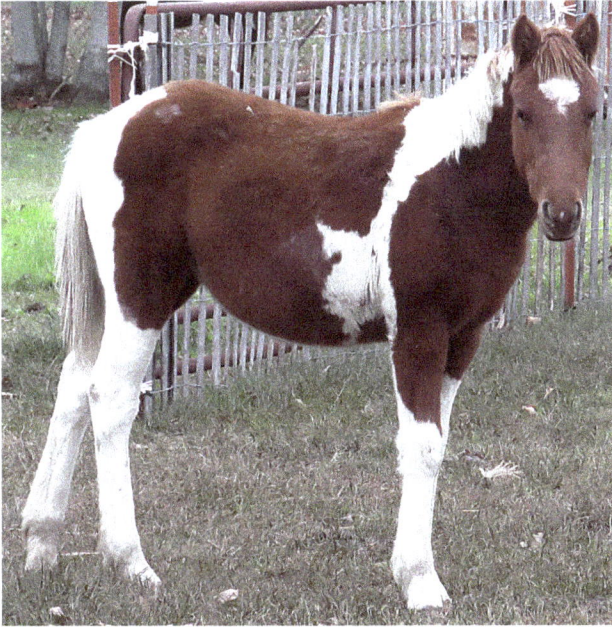

Chestnut Pinto

Anne Bonny

mare   brand: none
Yankee Spirit x Mystery

Notes:

_____

_____

_____

_____

_____

_____

_____

_____

_____

_____

Anne Bonny

Chestnut Pinto

Sweet Jane

Duckie
mare   brand: 06, partial

COURTNEY'S BOY x LEFTY'S CHECKMARK

Notes:

_____

_____

_____

_____

_____

_____

_____

_____

_____

_____

Sweet Jane

Chestnut Pinto

Little Duckie

Quackers
mare   brand: F
North Star x Sweet Jane

Notes:

_____

_____

_____

_____

_____

_____

_____

_____

_____

_____

_____

Little Duckie

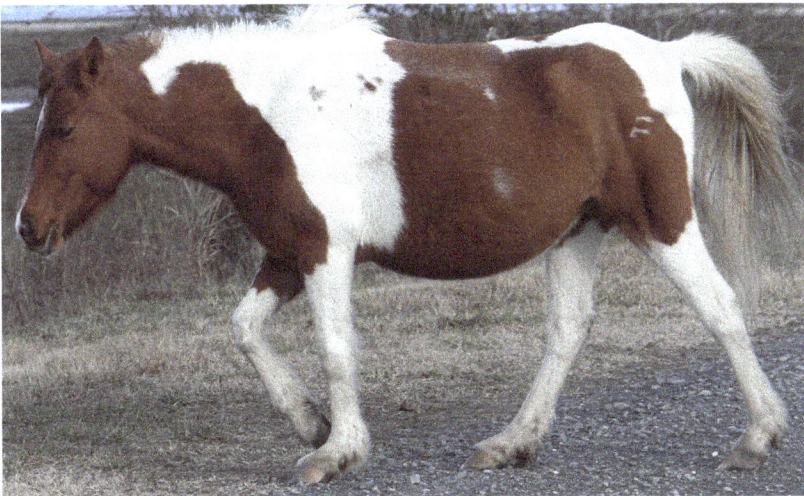

Chestnut Pinto

Misty Mills

mare   brand: 06, partial
COURTNEY'S BOY x SWEET MISCHIEF

Notes:

_____

_____

_____

_____

_____

_____

_____

_____

_____

_____

_____

Misty Mills

Chestnut Pinto

Beach Bunny

mare   brand: 15
ARCHER'S GAMBIT x SWEET JANE

Notes:

_____

_____

_____

_____

_____

_____

_____

_____

_____

_____

Beach Bunny

Chestnut Pinto

Archer's Gambit

Puzzle, Little Frog
stallion   brand: 08
NORTH STAR x LILY PAD

Notes:

_____

_____

_____

_____

_____

_____

_____

_____

_____

_____

_____

Archer's Gambit

Chestnut Pinto

Checkers

Giraffe
mare   brand: 7, partial
(UNKNOWN) x HITCH HIKER

Notes:

_____

_____

_____

_____

_____

_____

_____

_____

_____

_____

Checkers

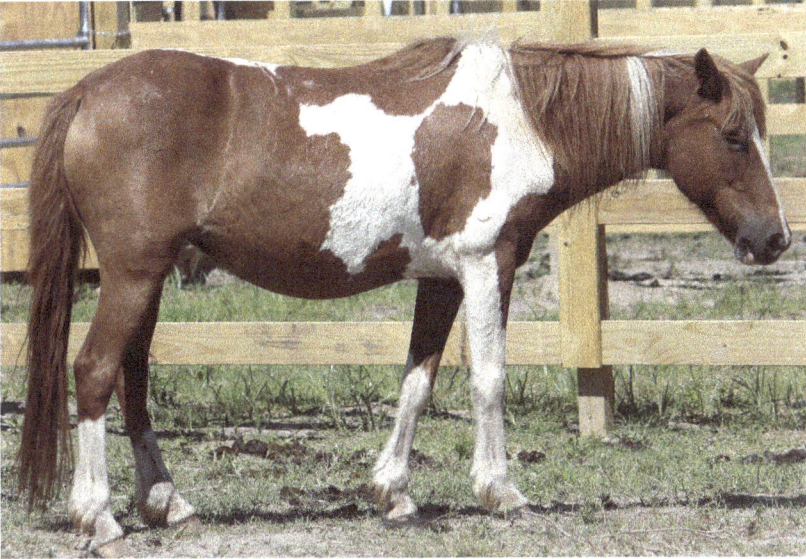

Chestnut Pinto

Stevenson's Dakota Sky

Dakota, Dakota Sky
mare   brand: 01
COURTNEY'S BOY x PROMISE OF SUMMER

Notes:

_____

_____

_____

_____

_____

_____

_____

_____

_____

_____

Stevenson's Dakota Sky

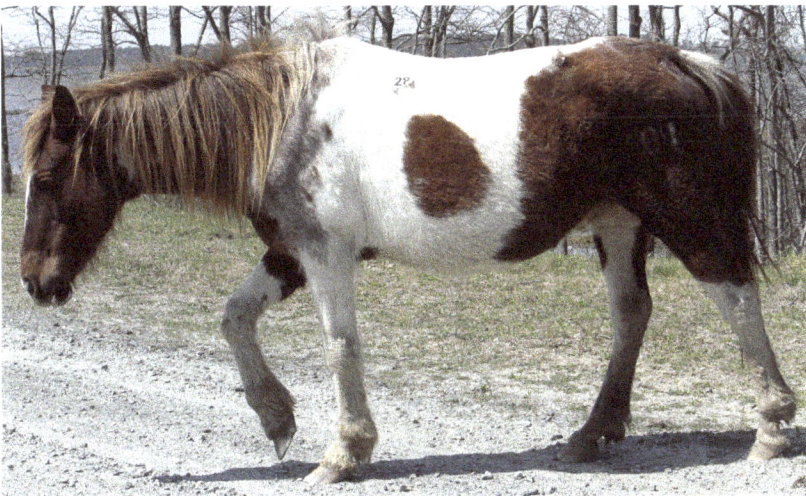

Chestnut Pinto

Courtney's Island Dove

Dove
mare   brand: unreadable
Courtney's Boy x Salt and Pepper

Notes:

_____

_____

_____

_____

_____

_____

_____

_____

_____

_____

Courtney's Island Dove

Chestnut Pinto

Little Bit O' Joansie

Joansie
mare   brand: 14
Courtney's Boy x Cinnamon Blaze

Notes:

_____

_____

_____

_____

_____

_____

_____

_____

_____

_____

Little Bit O' Joansie

Chestnut Pinto

Don Leonard Stud II

Lenny, Leonard Stud II
stallion   brand: 14
PHANTOM MIST x TUNIE

Notes:

_____

_____

_____

_____

_____

_____

_____

_____

_____

_____

_____

Don Leonard Stud II

Chestnut Pinto

Mary Read

mare   brand: 17
Tornado's Legacy x Anne Bonny

Notes:

_____

_____

_____

_____

_____

_____

_____

_____

_____

_____

Mary Read

Chestnut Pinto

Thetis

mare   brand: 01
Hot Air Balloon x Untouchable

Notes:

_____

_____

_____

_____

_____

_____

_____

_____

_____

_____

Thetis

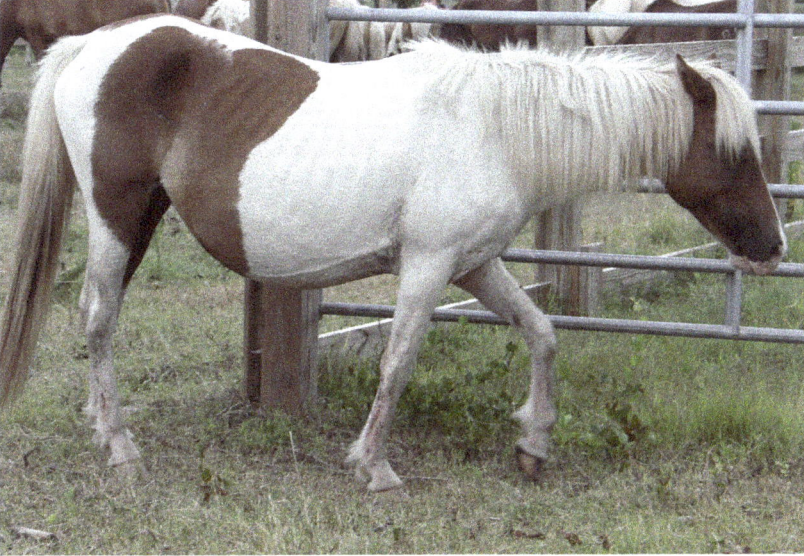

Chestnut Pinto

Sonny's Legacy

mare   brand: 13
LEONARD STUD x SHY ANNE

Notes:

_____

_____

_____

_____

_____

_____

_____

_____

_____

_____

_____

Sonny's Legacy

Chestnut Pinto

Gidget's Beach Baby

Beach Baby
mare   brand: none
North Star x Surfer Dude's Gidget

Notes:

_____

_____

_____

_____

_____

_____

_____

_____

_____

_____

_____

Gidget's Beach Baby

Chestnut Pinto

Wildfire

mare   brand: none
WH Nightwind x WH Sea Breeze

Notes:

_____

_____

_____

_____

_____

_____

_____

_____

_____

_____

Wildfire

Chestnut Pinto

Witch Kraft

Friendly Girl
mare   brand: none
(UNKNOWN) x WATERKOLOR

Notes:

Witch Kraft

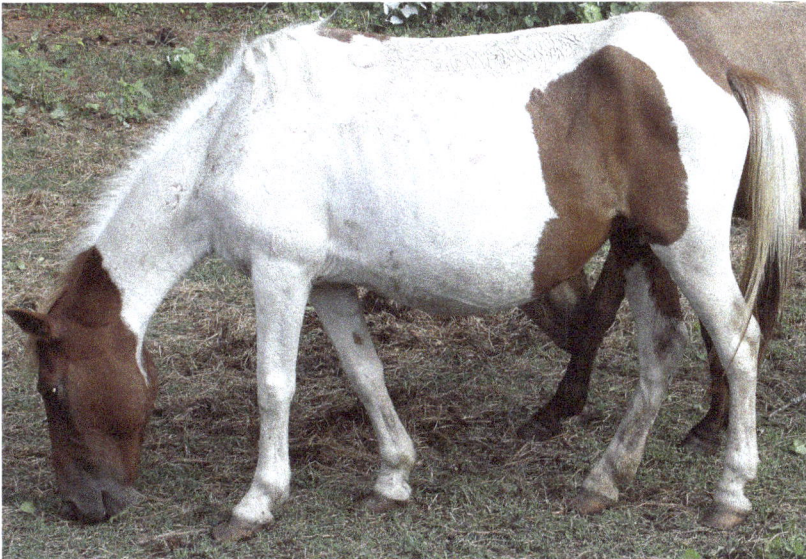

Chestnut Pinto

Thunderstorm Skies

Thunder
mare   brand: 13
Leonard Stud x Lily Pad

Notes:

_____

_____

_____

_____

_____

_____

_____

_____

_____

_____

Thunderstorm Skies

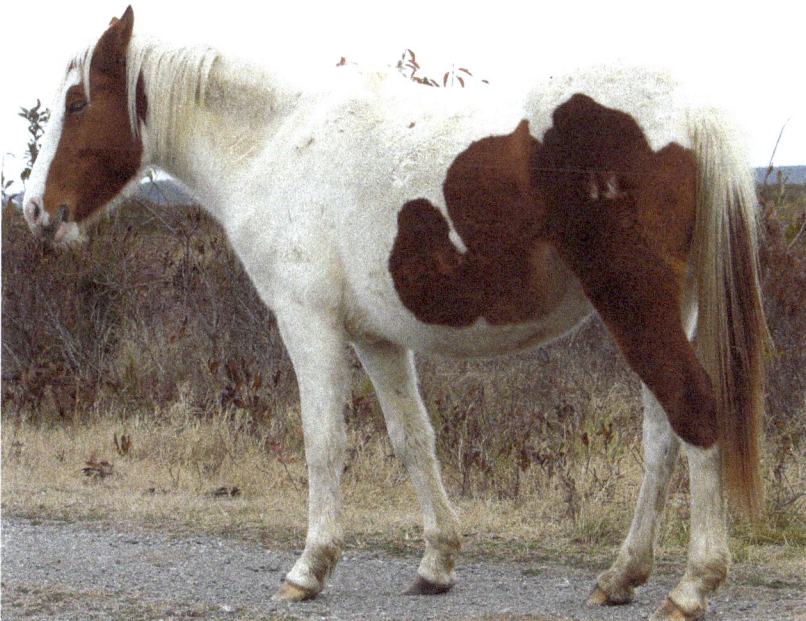

Chestnut Pinto

CLG Rumor Has It

Rumor
mare   brand: 18
KEN x WHISPER OF LIVING LEGEND

Notes:

_____

_____

_____

_____

_____

_____

_____

_____

_____

_____

Chestnut Pinto

CLG Rumor Has It

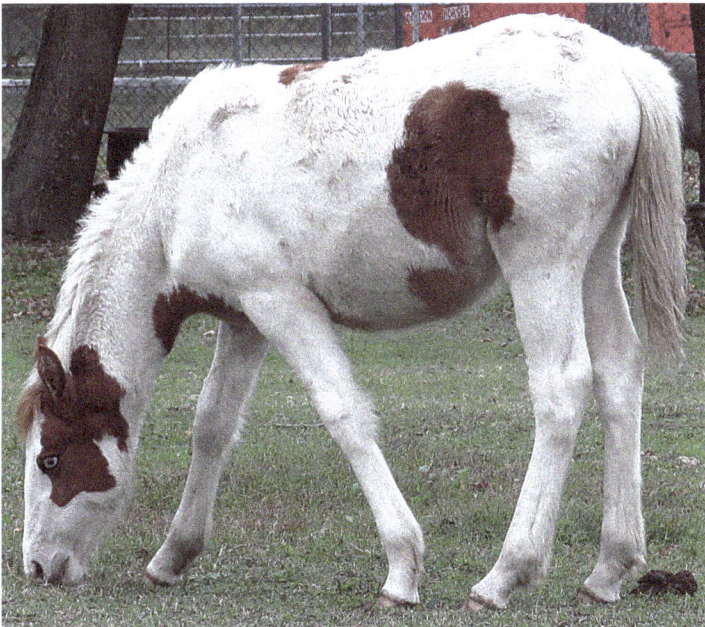

Palomino

CLG Cowboy Kisses

Cowboy Kisses
mare   brand: 17
CHIEF GOLDEN EAGLE X PONY LADIES' SWEET SURPRISE

Notes:

_____

_____

_____

_____

_____

_____

_____

_____

_____

_____

CLG Cowboy Kisses

Palomino

Chief Golden Eagle

Chief
stallion   brand: 08
GLACIER x BEAUTIFUL DREAMER

Notes:

_____

_____

_____

_____

_____

_____

_____

_____

_____

Chief Golden Eagle

Palomino

Kachina Mayli Mist

Mayli
mare   brand: 12

PHANTOM MIST x KACHINA GRAND STAR

Notes:

_____

_____

_____

_____

_____

_____

_____

_____

_____

_____

Kachina Mayli Mist

Palomino

Shy & Sassy Sweet Lady Suede

Suede
mare   brand: 14
CHIEF GOLDEN EAGLE x PONY LADIES' SWEET SURPRISE

Notes:

_____

_____

_____

_____

_____

_____

_____

_____

_____

_____

_____

Shy & Sassy Sweet Lady Suede

Palomino

Two Teague's Golden Girl

Goldie
mare   brand: 16
CHIEF GOLDEN EAGLE x TWO TEAGUES TACO

Notes:

_____

_____

_____

_____

_____

_____

_____

_____

_____

_____

Two Teague's Golden Girl

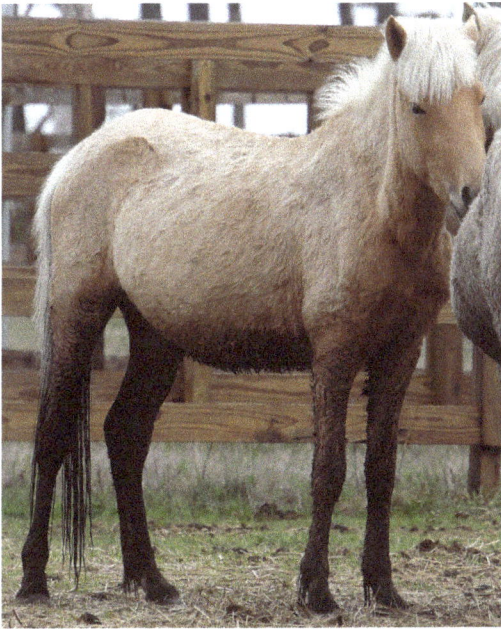

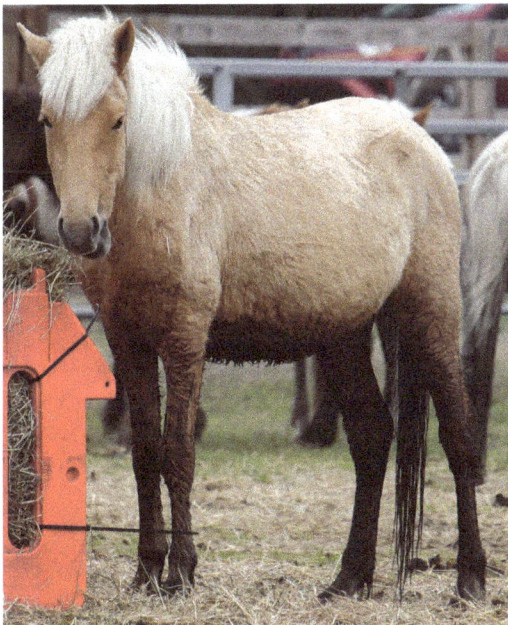

Palomino

Miss Admiral Halsey

mare   brand: 18
SURFER'S RIPTIDE x KACHINA MAYLI MIST

Notes:

_____

_____

_____

_____

_____

_____

_____

_____

_____

_____

Miss Admiral Halsey

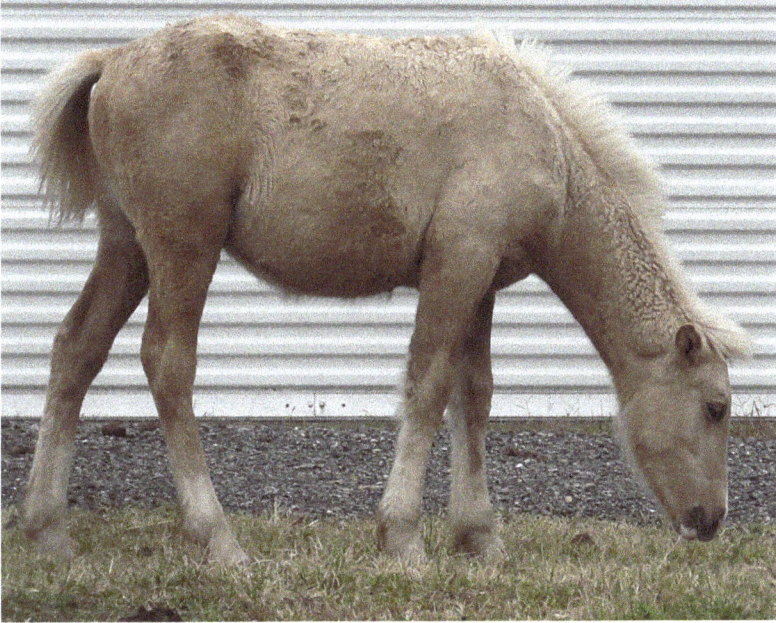

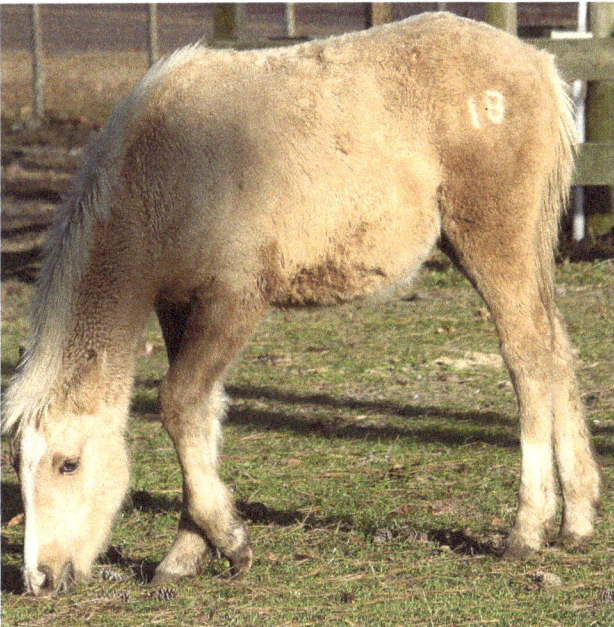

Palomino Comparison Chart

Name	Pg #	Brand	Mane	Face
CLG Cowboy Kisses	274	17	right	
Chief Golden Eagle	276	08	left	
Kachina Mayli Mist	278	12	left	
Miss Admiral Halsey	284	18	left	blaze
Shy & Sassy Sweet Lady Suede	280	14	split	
Two Teague's Golden Girl	282	16	left	

NOTES

Left & right refers to the animal's left & right.

Mane: left = falls to the left **right** = falls to the right **split** = significant portion falls on left and right

Palomino Comparison Chart

Legs				Notable Details
R F	**R B**	**L F**	**L B**	
				stallion; long forelock
				pale coat; short hairs stand up along neck like a mohawk
sock	sock	sock	sock	only one with white on face and legs

R F = right front   **R B** = right back **L F** = left front   **L B** = left back
sock = white well below the knee   **stocking** = white near and above the knee

baldface = white covers most of the face   **blaze** = white streak running down the length of the face   **snip** = white spot on the muzzle   **star** = white spot on the forehead

Palomino Pinto

Tornado's Prince of Tides

Prince
stallion   brand: 07
TORNADO x SAND CHERRY

Notes:

_____

_____

_____

_____

_____

_____

_____

_____

_____

_____

Tornado's Prince of Tides

Palomino Pinto

Judy's Sunshine

Wings
mare   brand: 18
Tornado's Prince of Tides x Catwalk Chaos

Notes:

_____

_____

_____

_____

_____

_____

_____

_____

_____

_____

Judy's Sunshine

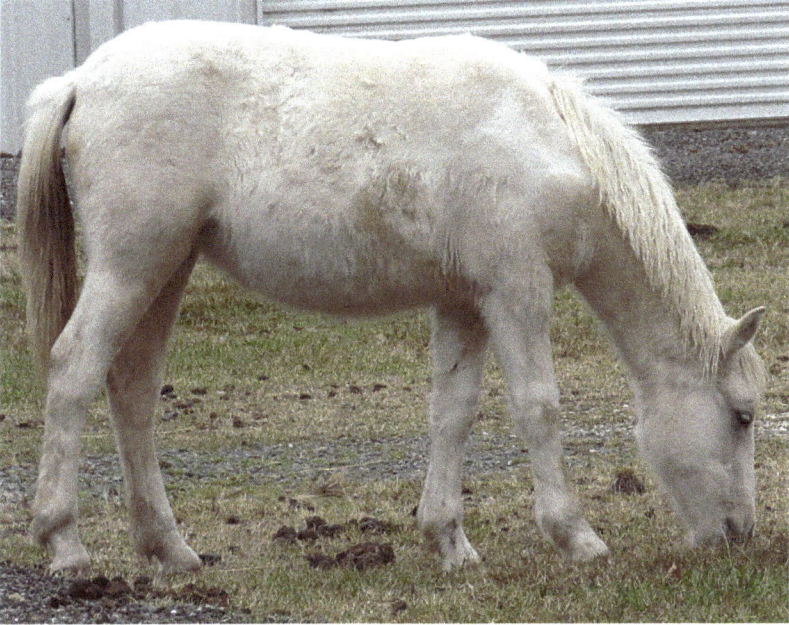

Palomino Pinto

Little Miss Sunshine

Sunshine
mare   brand: 15
TORNADO'S PRINCE OF TIDES x BAYBE

Notes:

_____

_____

_____

_____

_____

_____

_____

_____

_____

_____

Little Miss Sunshine

Palomino Pinto

Whisper of Living Legend

Whisper
mare   brand: 00
NORTH STAR x LIVING LEGEND

Notes:

_____

_____

_____

_____

_____

_____

_____

_____

_____

_____

_____

Whisper of Living Legend

Palomino Pinto

Jigsaw's Little Miss Skeeter

Skeeter
mare   brand: 18
Tornado's Legacy x Cody's Little Jigsaw Puzzle

Notes:

_____

_____

_____

_____

_____

_____

_____

_____

_____

_____

Jigsaw's Little Miss Skeeter

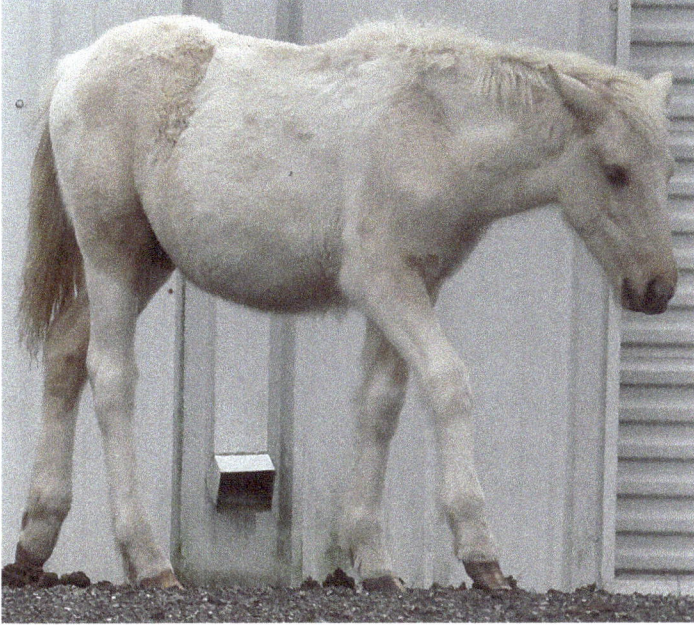

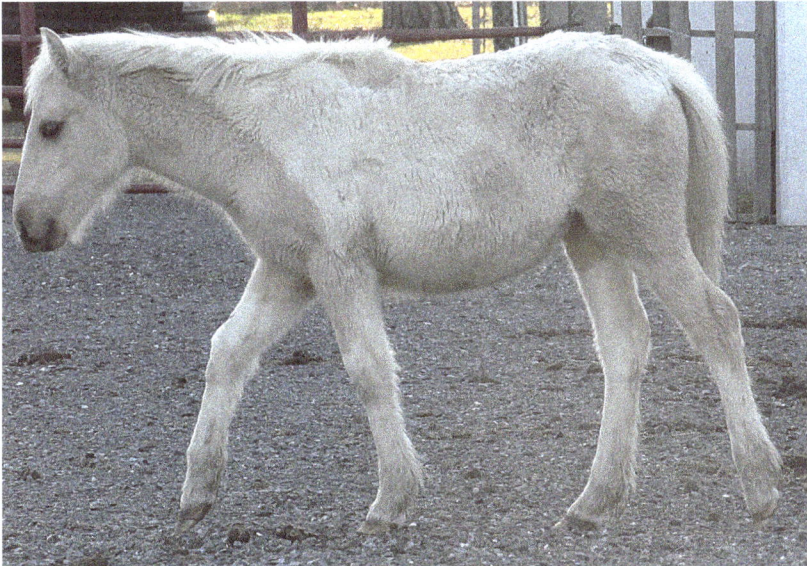

Palomino Pinto

Sundance

mare   brand: none
WH Nightwind x (unknown)

Notes:

_____
_____
_____
_____
_____
_____
_____

_____
_____
_____
_____

Sundance

Palomino Pinto

Marina's Marsh Mallow

Marsh Mallow
mare   brand: 14
TORNADO'S PRINCE OF TIDES X FIFTEEN FRIENDS OF FRECKLES

Notes:

Marina's Marsh Mallow

Palomino Pinto

Lorna Dune

mare   brand: 13
LEONARD STUD x JESSICA'S SEA STAR SANDY

Notes:

_____

_____

_____

_____

_____

_____

_____

_____

_____

_____

_____

Lorna Dune

Close Family Index

In order to save space, the relationship of an entry in this index is identified by font and color.

Color Key

Name - Bold Black
Sire - Small Caps Blue
Dam - Small Caps Pink
Offspring - Green
Sibling Same Sire - Italics Blue
Sibling Same Dam - Italics Pink
Sibling Same Sire & Dam - Italics Black

A Splash of Freckles, 102

FIFTEEN FRIENDS OF FRECKLES, 90 *Heide's Sky*, 108 *Lorna Dune*, 302 *Marina's Marsh Mallow*, 300 *Poco's Starry Night*, 122 *Sonny's Legacy*, 262 *Thunderstorm Skies*, 270

Ace's Black Tie Affair, 120

SUSIE Q, 230 Carli Marie, 234 Pixie Dust, 124

Ajax, 56

Catwalk's Olympic Glory, 212 MissMe, 58 Rosie's Teapot, 34 *Anne Bonny*, 236 *Ella of Assateague*, 38 *Molly's Rosebud*, 156 *Skylark*, 92

Alice's Sandcastle, 136

Archer's Gambit, 246 *CJ SAMM'N*, 220 *Fifteen Friends of Freckles*, 90 *Gidget's Beach Baby*, 264 *Kachina Grand Star*, 152 *Kimball's Rainbow Delight*, 222 *Little Duckie*, 240 **Whisper of Living Legend**, 294

Anne Bonny, 236

Mary Read, 258 *Ajax*, 56 *Molly's Rosebud*, 156

Archer's Gambit, 246

Beach Bunny, 244 Marguerite of Chincoteague, 86 *Alice's Sandcastle*, 136 *CJ SAMM'N*, 220 *Fifteen Friends of Freckles*, 90 *Gidget's Beach Baby*, 264 *Kachina Grand Star*, 152 *Kimball's Rainbow Delight*, 222 *Little Duckie*, 240 *Thunderstorm Skies*, 270 *Whisper of Living Legend*, 294

Babe, 60

Bay Girl, 4 *Black Star*, 84 *Got Milk*, 106 *Slash of White*, 216 *Two Teagues Taco*, 18 *White Saddle*, 44

Badabing, 160

TORNADO'S PRINCE OF TIDES, 288 ELLA OF ASSATEAGUE, 38 *CLG Bay Princess*, 158 *Cody's Little Jigsaw Puzzle*, 40 *Judy's Sunshine*, 290 *Little Miss Sunshine*, 292 *Marina's Marsh Mallow*, 300 *Randy*, 166

Bay Girl, 4

Babe, 60 *Black Star*, 84 *Got Milk*, 106 *Slash of White*, 216 **Two Teagues Taco**, 18 **White Saddle**, 44

Close Family Index

Baybe, 130
CLG Bay Princess, 158 Little Miss Sunshine, 292 Randy, 166

Beach Boy, 134
Calendar Girl, 132 Summer, 98 Sundance, 298 *Wildfire*, 266

Beach Bunny, 244
ARCHER'S GAMBIT, 246 SWEET JANE, 238 Little Duckie, 240
Marguerite of Chincoteague, 86

Black Pearl, 128
LEAH'S BAYSIDE ANGEL, 24 CLG Ember, 110 Effie's Papa Bear,
10 *Gracey*, 126 **Jean Bonde's Bayside Angel**, 22 Milly Sue, 114

Black Star, 84
Chickadee, 80 Scotty ET, 94 Babe, 60 Bay Girl, 4 Got Milk,
106 Slash of White, 216 Two Teagues Taco, 18 White Saddle, 44

Bling Bling, 30
TORNADO'S LEGACY, 164 UNFORGETTABLE 2001, 192 CLG
ToMorrow's Tidewater Twist, 162 Jigsaw's Little Miss Skeeter, 296
Mary Read, 258

Calendar Girl, 132
Beach Boy, 134 Summer, 98 Sundance, 298 Wildfire, 266

Carli Marie, 234
ACE'S BLACK TIE AFFAIR, 120 GIDGET'S BEACH BABY, 264
Pixie Dust, 124

Carol's Little Freedom, 50
Pony Girl's Bliss, 228 Unforgettable 2001, 192 Wild Thing, 78

Catwalk Chaos, 232
Catwalk's Olympic Glory, 212 Judy's Sunshine, 290

Catwalk's Olympic Glory, 212
AJAX, 56 CATWALK CHAOS, 232 Judy's Sunshine, 290 MissMe,
58 Rosie's Teapot, 34

Checkers, 248

Chickadee, 80
BLACK STAR, 84 Courtney's Island Dove, 252 Destiny Feathering
Spirit, 66 Sweet Jane, 238 Kimmee-Sue, 186 Little Bit O' Joansie,
254 Misty Mills, 242 Scotty ET, 94 Stevenson's Dakota Sky, 250

Chief Golden Eagle, 276
Chili, 214 CLG Cowboy Kisses, 274 Shy & Sassy Sweet Lady Suede, 280 Two Teague's Golden Girl, 282

Chili, 214
CHIEF GOLDEN EAGLE, 276 CLG Cowboy Kisses, 274 Shy & Sassy Sweet Lady Suede, 280 Two Teague's Golden Girl, 282

Cinnamon Blaze, 184
Kimmee-Sue, 186 Little Bit O' Joansie, 254

CJ SAMM'N, 220
SLASH OF WHITE, 216 Alice's Sandcastle, 136 Archer's Gambit, 246 Fifteen Friends of Freckles, 90 Gidget's Beach Baby, 264 Kachina Grand Star, 152 Kimball's Rainbow Delight, 222 Little Duckie, 240 Whisper of Living Legend, 294

CLG Bay Princess, 158
TORNADO'S PRINCE OF TIDES, 288 BAYBE, 130 Badabing, 160 Cody's Little Jigsaw Puzzle, 40 Judy's Sunshine, 290 Little Miss Sunshine, 292 Marina's Marsh Mallow, 300 Randy, 166

CLG Cowboy Kisses, 274
CHIEF GOLDEN EAGLE, 276 PONY LADIES' SWEET SURPRISE, 16 Chili, 214 Shy & Sassy Sweet Lady Suede, 280 Two Teague's Golden Girl, 282

CLG Ember, 110
SURFER'S RIPTIDE, 208 BLACK PEARL, 128 Judy's Little Smooch, 194 Milly Sue, 114 Miss Admiral Halsey, 284

CLG Rumor Has It, 272
KEN, 204 WHISPER OF LIVING LEGEND, 294 Dreamer's Stardust, 206 Heide's Sky, 108

CLG Surfer's Blue Moon, 116
GOT MILK, 106 Dreamer's Gift, 198 Surfer Dude's Gidget, 196 Surfer's Riptide, 208 Surfer Princess, 200 Surfer's Shining Star, 174 Surfin' Scarlet, 188

CLG ToMorrow's Tidewater Twist, 162
TORNADO'S LEGACY, 164 SWEETHEART, 68 Bling Bling, 30 Jigsaw's Little Miss Skeeter, 296 Mary Read, 258

Close Family Index

Cody's Little Jigsaw Puzzle, 40
TORNADO'S PRINCE OF TIDES, 288 DAKOTA SKY'S CODY
TWO SOCKS, 28 Jigsaw's Little Miss Skeeter, 296 *Badabing*,
160 *CLG Bay Princess*, 158 *Doctor Amrien*, 42 *Judy's Sunshine*,
290 *Little Miss Sunshine*, 292 *Marina's Marsh Mallow*, 300 *Randy*,
166

Courtney's Island Dove, 252
Chickadee, 80 *Destiny Feathering Spirit*, 66 *Sweet Jane*, 238
Kimmee-Sue, 186 *Little Bit O' Joansie*, 254 *Misty Mills*, 242
Stevenson's Dakota Sky, 250

Daisey, 6
Ella of Assateague, 38 *Molly's Rosebud*, 156 **Too Grand**, 150

Dakota Sky's Cody Two Socks, 28
STEVENSON'S DAKOTA SKY, 250 Cody's Little Jigsaw Puzzle,
40 Doctor Amrien, 42

Destiny Feathering Spirit, 66
Chickadee, 80 *Courtney's Island Dove*, 252 *Sweet Jane*, 238
Kimmee-Sue, 186 *Little Bit O' Joansie*, 254 *Misty Mills*, 242
Stevenson's Dakota Sky, 250 *Susie Q*, 230

Doc's Bay Dream, 8
EFFIE'S PAPA BEAR, 10 DOCTOR AMRIEN, 42 *Pony Girl's
Bliss*, 228 *Tawny Treasure*, 26

Doctor Amrien, 42
WILD THING, 78 DAKOTA SKY'S CODY TWO SOCKS, 28
Doc's Bay Dream, 8 *Cody's Little Jigsaw Puzzle*, 40 *Splash*, 72
Grandma's Dream, 74 *Henry's Hidalgo*, 70 *Ken*, 204 *Loveland's
Secret Feather*, 76 *Maverick*, 104 *Skylark*, 92

Don Leonard Stud II, 256
TUNIE, 52 *Kachina Mayli Mist*, 278 *Precious Jewel*, 190

Dreamer's Gift, 198
Dreamer's Stardust, 206 *CLG Surfer's Blue Moon*, 116 *Surfer
Dude's Gidget*, 196 *Surfer's Riptide*, 208 *Surfer Princess*, 200
Surfer's Shining Star, 174 *Surfin' Scarlet*, 188

Dreamer's Stardust, 206
KEN, 204 DREAMER'S GIFT, 198 CLG Rumor Has It, 272 Heide's Sky, 108

Effie's Papa Bear, 10
Doc's Bay Dream, 8 Pony Girl's Bliss, 228 Tawny Treasure, 26 Black Pearl, 128 Gracey, 126 Jean Bonde's Bayside Angel, 22

Ella of Assateague, 38
Badabing, 160 Ajax, 56 Daisey, 6 Too Grand, 150 Skylark, 92

Fifteen Friends of Freckles, 90
A Splash of Freckles, 102 Heide's Sky, 108 Marina's Marsh Mallow, 300 Alice's Sandcastle, 136 Archer's Gambit, 246 CJ SAMM'N, 220 Gidget's Beach Baby, 264 Kachina Grand Star, 152 Kimball's Rainbow Delight, 222 Little Duckie, 240 Whisper of Living Legend, 294

Gidget's Beach Baby, 264
SURFER DUDE'S GIDGET, 196 Carli Marie, 234 Alice's Sandcastle, 136 Archer's Gambit, 246 CJ SAMM'N, 220 Fifteen Friends of Freckles, 90 Kachina Grand Star, 152 Kimball's Rainbow Delight, 222 Little Duckie, 240 Whisper of Living Legend, 294

Good Ole Days Bailey's Star, 224

Got Milk, 106
CLG Surfer's Blue Moon, 116 Babe, 60 Bay Girl, 4 Black Star, 84 Slash of White, 216 Two Teagues Taco, 18 White Saddle, 44 Witch Kraft, 268

Gracey, 126
LEAH'S BAYSIDE ANGEL, 24 Black Pearl, 128 Effie's Papa Bear, 10 Jean Bonde's Bayside Angel, 22 Milly Sue, 114

Grandma's Dream, 74
WILD THING, 78 Splash, 72 Doctor Amrien, 42 Henry's Hidalgo, 70 Ken, 204 Loveland's Secret Feather, 76 Maverick, 104 Skylark, 92

Close Family Index

Heide's Sky, 108
KEN, 204 FIFTEEN FRIENDS OF FRECKLES, 90 *A Splash of Freckles*, 102 *CLG Rumor Has It*, 272 *Dreamer's Stardust*, 206 *Marina's Marsh Mallow*, 300

Henry's Hidalgo, 70
WILD THING, 78 THETIS, 260 *Splash*, 72 *Doctor Amrien*, 42 *Grandma's Dream*, 74 *Ken*, 204 *Loveland's Secret Feather*, 76 *Maverick*, 104 *Skylark*, 92

Ivana Marie Zustan, 138
LITTLE DOLPHIN, 12 JESSICA'S SEA STAR SANDY, 140 *Lorna Dune*, 302 **Sunrise Ocean Tides**, 148

JABATAA, 172
Lefty's Checkmark, 218 *Susana*, 178 *Suzy's Sweetheart*, 180 *Tidewater Treasure*, 170 *Tuleta Star*, 182 *Tiger Lily*, 226

Jean Bonde's Bayside Angel, 22
LEAH'S BAYSIDE ANGEL, 24 **Black Pearl**, 128 *Effie's Papa Bear*, 10 **Gracey**, 126 *Milly Sue*, 114

Jessica's Sea Star Sandy, 140
Ivana Marie Zustan, 138 Lorna Dune, 302 Sunrise Ocean Tides, 148 **Landrie's Georgia Peach**, 142 *Tornado's Legacy*, 164 *Tornado's Prince of Tides*, 288

Jigsaw's Little Miss Skeeter, 296
TORNADO'S LEGACY, 164 CODY'S LITTLE JIGSAW PUZZLE, 40 *Bling Bling*, 30 *CLG ToMorrow's Tidewater Twist*, 162 *Mary Read*, 258

Judy's Little Smooch, 194
SURFER'S RIPTIDE, 208 *CLG Ember*, 110 *Milly Sue*, 114 *Miss Admiral Halsey*, 284

Judy's Sunshine, 290
TORNADO'S PRINCE OF TIDES, 288 CATWALK CHAOS, 232 *Badabing*, 160 *Catwalk's Olympic Glory*, 212 *CLG Bay Princess*, 158 *Cody's Little Jigsaw Puzzle*, 40 *Little Miss Sunshine*, 292 *Marina's Marsh Mallow*, 300 *Randy*, 166

Kachina Grand Star, 152
TOO GRAND, 150 Kachina Mayli Mist, 278 Alice's Sandcastle, 136 Archer's Gambit, 246 CJ SAMM'N, 220 Fifteen Friends of Freckles, 90 Gidget's Beach Baby, 264 Kimball's Rainbow Delight, 222 Little Duckie, 240 Whisper of Living Legend, 294

Kachina Mayli Mist, 278
KACHINA GRAND STAR, 152 Miss Admiral Halsey, 284 Don Leonard Stud II, 256 Precious Jewel, 190

Ken, 204
WILD THING, 78 CLG Rumor Has It, 272 Dreamer's Stardust, 206 Heide's Sky, 108 Splash, 72 Doctor Amrien, 42 Grandma's Dream, 74 Henry's Hidalgo, 70 Loveland's Secret Feather, 76 Maverick, 104 Skylark, 92

Kimball's Rainbow Delight, 222
Alice's Sandcastle, 136 Archer's Gambit, 246 CJ SAMM'N, 220 Fifteen Friends of Freckles, 90 Gidget's Beach Baby, 264 Kachina Grand Star, 152 Little Duckie, 240 Whisper of Living Legend, 294

Kimmee-Sue, 186
CINNAMON BLAZE, 184 Chickadee, 80 Courtney's Island Dove, 252 Destiny Feathering Spirit, 66 Sweet Jane, 238 Little Bit O' Joansie, 254 Misty Mills, 242 Stevenson's Dakota Sky, 250

Landrie's Georgia Peach, 142
Little Dolphin, 12 Liz's Serenity, 144 Jessica's Sea Star Sandy, 140 Tornado's Legacy, 164 Tornado's Prince of Tides, 288

Leah's Bayside Angel, 24
Black Pearl, 128 Gracey, 126 Jean Bonde's Bayside Angel, 22 Milly Sue, 114 Pappy's Pony, 14

Lefty's Checkmark, 218
Sweet Jane, 238 JABATAA, 172 Susana, 178 Suzy's Sweetheart, 180 Tidewater Treasure, 170 Tuleta Star, 182 Tiger Lily, 226

Little Bit O' Joansie, 254
CINNAMON BLAZE, 184 Chickadee, 80 Courtney's Island Dove, 252 Destiny Feathering Spirit, 66 Sweet Jane, 238 Kimmee-Sue, 186 Misty Mills, 242 Stevenson's Dakota Sky, 250

Close Family Index

Little Dolphin, 12

RAINBOW WARRIOR, 64 LANDRIE'S GEORGIA PEACH, 142
Ivana Marie Zustan, 138 Sunrise Ocean Tides, 148 Liz's
Serenity, 144 Surfin' Chantel, 176

Little Duckie, 240

SWEET JANE, 238 Alice's Sandcastle, 136 Archer's Gambit, 246
Beach Bunny, 244 CJ SAMM'N, 220 Fifteen Friends of Freckles,
90 Gidget's Beach Baby, 264 Kachina Grand Star, 152 Kimball's
Rainbow Delight, 222 Whisper of Living Legend, 294

Little Miss Sunshine, 292

TORNADO'S PRINCE OF TIDES, 288 BAYBE, 130 Badabing, 160
CLG Bay Princess, 158 Cody's Little Jigsaw Puzzle, 40 Judy's
Sunshine, 290 Marina's Marsh Mallow, 300 Randy, 166

Liz's Serenity, 144

LANDRIE'S GEORGIA PEACH, 142 Little Dolphin, 12 Sweetheart,
68

Lorna Dune, 302

JESSICA'S SEA STAR SANDY, 140 A Splash of Freckles, 102 Ivana
Marie Zustan, 138 Poco's Starry Night, 122 Sonny's Legacy, 262
Sunrise Ocean Tides, 148 Thunderstorm Skies, 270

Loveland's Secret Feather, 76

WILD THING, 78 Splash, 72 Doctor Amrien, 42 Grandma's
Dream, 74 Henry's Hidalgo, 70 Ken, 204 Maverick, 104 Skylark,
92

Marguerite of Chincoteague, 86

ARCHER'S GAMBIT, 246 MIRACLE'S NATURAL BEAUTY, 46
Beach Bunny, 244 MissMe, 58

Marina's Marsh Mallow, 300

TORNADO'S PRINCE OF TIDES, 288 FIFTEEN FRIENDS OF
FRECKLES, 90 A Splash of Freckles, 102 Badabing, 160 CLG Bay
Princess, 158 Cody's Little Jigsaw Puzzle, 40 Heide's Sky, 108
Judy's Sunshine, 290 Little Miss Sunshine, 292 Randy, 166

Mary Read, 258
TORNADO'S LEGACY, 164 ANNE BONNY, 236 *Bling Bling*, 30
CLG ToMorrow's Tidewater Twist, 162 *Jigsaw's Little Miss Skeeter*, 296

Maverick, 104
WILD THING, 78 WITCH KRAFT, 268 Talia/Evan's Angel, 112
Serendipity, 168 Wendy's Carolina Girl, 54 *Splash*, 72 *Doctor Amrien*, 42 *Grandma's Dream*, 74 *Henry's Hidalgo*, 70 *Ken*, 204
Loveland's Secret Feather, 76 *Skylark*, 92

May's Grand Slam, 48
Millennium Midnight, 62 *Miracle's Natural Beauty*, 46 *Seaside Miracle*, 100 *Summer Breeze*, 36 *Wildest Dreams*, 82

Millennium Midnight, 62
May's Grand Slam, 48 *Miracle's Natural Beauty*, 46 *Seaside Miracle*, 100 *Summer Breeze*, 36 *Wildest Dreams*, 82

Milly Sue, 114
SURFER'S RIPTIDE, 208 LEAH'S BAYSIDE ANGEL, 24 *Black Pearl*, 128 *CLG Ember*, 110 *Gracey*, 126 *Jean Bonde's Bayside Angel*, 22 *Judy's Little Smooch*, 194 *Miss Admiral Halsey*, 284

Miracle's Natural Beauty, 46
Marguerite of Chincoteague, 86 MissMe, 58 *May's Grand Slam*, 48 *Millennium Midnight*, 62 *Seaside Miracle*, 100 *Summer Breeze*, 36 **Wildest Dreams**, 82

Miss Admiral Halsey, 284
SURFER'S RIPTIDE, 208 KACHINA MAYLI MIST, 278 *CLG Ember*, 110 *Judy's Little Smooch*, 194 *Milly Sue*, 114

MissMe, 58
AJAX, 56 MIRACLE'S NATURAL BEAUTY, 46 *Catwalk's Olympic Glory*, 212 *Marguerite of Chincoteague*, 86 *Rosie's Teapot*, 34

Misty Mills, 242
Chickadee, 80 *Courtney's Island Dove*, 252 *Destiny Feathering Spirit*, 66 *Sweet Jane*, 238 *Kimmee-Sue*, 186 *Little Bit O' Joansie*, 254 *Slash of White*, 216 *Stevenson's Dakota Sky*, 250

Close Family Index

Molly's Rosebud, 156
Rosie's Teapot, 34 Ajax, 56 Anne Bonny, 236 Daisey, 6 Too Grand, 150

Pappy's Pony, 14
Leah's Bayside Angel, 24

Pixie Dust, 124
Ace's Black Tie Affair, 120 Carli Marie, 234

Poco Latte PW, 146
Poco's Starry Night, 122 Pony Ladies' Sweet Surprise, 16

Poco's Starry Night, 122
Poco Latte PW, 146 A Splash of Freckles, 102 Lorna Dune, 302 Sonny's Legacy, 262 Thunderstorm Skies, 270

Pony Girl's Bliss, 228
Effie's Papa Bear, 10 Carol's Little Freedom, 50 Doc's Bay Dream, 8 Tawny Treasure, 26

Pony Ladies' Sweet Surprise, 16
CLG Cowboy Kisses, 274 Shy & Sassy Sweet Lady Suede, 280 Poco Latte PW, 146

Precious Jewel, 190
Unci, 20 Kachina Mayli Mist, 278 Don Leonard Stud II, 256 Tornado's Legacy, 164

Rainbow Warrior, 64
Little Dolphin, 12 Surfin' Chantel, 176

Randy, 166
Tornado's Prince of Tides, 288 Baybe, 130 Badabing, 160 CLG Bay Princess, 158 Cody's Little Jigsaw Puzzle, 40 Judy's Sunshine, 290 Little Miss Sunshine, 292 Marina's Marsh Mallow, 300

Rosie's Teapot, 34
Ajax, 56 Molly's Rosebud, 156 Catwalk's Olympic Glory, 212 MissMe, 58

Scotty ET, 94
Black Star, 84 Sweetheart, 68 Chickadee, 80

Seaside Miracle, 100
May's Grand Slam, 48 *Millennium Midnight*, 62 *Miracle's Natural Beauty*, 46 *Summer Breeze*, 36 *Tunie*, 52 *Wildest Dreams*, 82

Serendipity, 168
Maverick, 104 *Talia/Evan's Angel*, 112 *Wendy's Carolina Girl*, 54

Shy & Sassy Sweet Lady Suede, 280
Chief Golden Eagle, 276 **Pony Ladies' Sweet Surprise**, 16 *Chili*, 214 **CLG Cowboy Kisses**, 274 *Two Teague's Golden Girl*, 282

Shy Anne, 88
Sonny's Legacy, 262 *Thetis*, 260

Skylark, 92
Wild Thing, 78 *Ajax*, 56 *Splash*, 72 *Doctor Amrien*, 42 *Ella of Assateague*, 38 *Grandma's Dream*, 74 *Henry's Hidalgo*, 70 *Ken*, 204 *Loveland's Secret Feather*, 76 *Maverick*, 104

Slash of White, 216
CJ SAMM'N, 220 *Babe*, 60 *Bay Girl*, 4 *Black Star*, 84 *Got Milk*, 106 *Misty Mills*, 242 *Two Teagues Taco*, 18 *White Saddle*, 44

Sonny's Legacy, 262
Shy Anne, 88 *A Splash of Freckles*, 102 *Lorna Dune*, 302 *Poco's Starry Night*, 122 *Thunderstorm Skies*, 270

Splash, 72
Wild Thing, 78 **Summer Breeze**, 36 *Doctor Amrien*, 42 *Grandma's Dream*, 74 *Henry's Hidalgo*, 70 *Ken*, 204 *Loveland's Secret Feather*, 76 *Maverick*, 104 *Skylark*, 92

Stevenson's Dakota Sky, 250
Dakota Sky's Cody Two Socks, 28 *Chickadee*, 80 *Courtney's Island Dove*, 252 *Destiny Feathering Spirit*, 66 *Sweet Jane*, 238 *Kimmee-Sue*, 186 *Little Bit O' Joansie*, 254 *Misty Mills*, 242

Summer, 98
Beach Boy, 134 *Calendar Girl*, 132 *Sundance*, 298 *Wildfire*, 266

Close Family Index

Summer Breeze, 36
Splash, 72 *May's Grand Slam*, 48 *Millennium Midnight*, 62 *Miracle's Natural Beauty*, 46 *Seaside Miracle*, 100 *Wildest Dreams*, 82

Sundance, 298
Surfette, 202 *Beach Boy*, 134 *Calendar Girl*, 132 *Summer*, 98 *Wildfire*, 266

Sunrise Ocean Tides, 148
LITTLE DOLPHIN, 12 JESSICA'S SEA STAR SANDY, 140 *Ivana Marie Zustan*, 138 *Lorna Dune*, 302

Surfer Dude's Gidget, 196
Gidget's Beach Baby, 264 *CLG Surfer's Blue Moon*, 116 *Dreamer's Gift*, 198 *Surfer's Riptide*, 208 *Surfer Princess*, 200 *Surfer's Shining Star*, 174 *Surfin' Scarlet*, 188

Surfer Princess, 200
CLG Surfer's Blue Moon, 116 *Dreamer's Gift*, 198 *Surfer Dude's Gidget*, 196 **Surfer's Riptide**, 208 *Surfer's Shining Star*, 174 **Surfin' Scarlet**, 188

Surfer's Riptide, 208
CLG Ember, 110 Judy's Little Smooch, 194 Milly Sue, 114 Miss Admiral Halsey, 284 *CLG Surfer's Blue Moon*, 116 *Dreamer's Gift*, 198 *Surfer Dude's Gidget*, 196 **Surfer Princess**, 200 *Surfer's Shining Star*, 174 **Surfin' Scarlet**, 188

Surfer's Shining Star, 174
CLG Surfer's Blue Moon, 116 *Dreamer's Gift*, 198 *Surfer Dude's Gidget*, 196 *Surfer's Riptide*, 208 *Surfer Princess*, 200 *Surfin' Scarlet*, 188

Surfette, 202
SUNDANCE, 298

Surfin' Chantel, 176
RAINBOW WARRIOR, 64 SURFIN' SCARLET, 188 Talia/Evan's Angel, 112 *Little Dolphin*, 12

Surfin' Scarlet, 188
Surfin' Chantel, 176 CLG Surfer's Blue Moon, 116 Dreamer's Gift, 198 Surfer Dude's Gidget, 196 **Surfer's Riptide**, 208 **Surfer Princess**, 200 Surfer's Shining Star, 174

Susana, 178
JABATAA, 172 Lefty's Checkmark, 218 Suzy's Sweetheart, 180 Tidewater Treasure, 170 Tuleta Star, 182 Tiger Lily, 226

Susie Q, 230
Ace's Black Tie Affair, 120 Destiny Feathering Spirit, 66

Suzy's Sweetheart, 180
JABATAA, 172 Lefty's Checkmark, 218 Susana, 178 Tidewater Treasure, 170 Tuleta Star, 182 **Tiger Lily**, 226

Sweet Jane, 238
LEFTY'S CHECKMARK, 218 Beach Bunny, 244 Little Duckie, 240 Chickadee, 80 Courtney's Island Dove, 252 Destiny Feathering Spirit, 66 Kimmee-Sue, 186 Little Bit O' Joansie, 254 Misty Mills, 242 Stevenson's Dakota Sky, 250

Sweetheart, 68
SCOTTY ET, 94 CLG ToMorrow's Tidewater Twist, 162 Liz's Serenity, 144

Talia/Evan's Angel, 112
MAVERICK, 104 SURFIN' CHANTEL, 176 Serendipity, 168 Wendy's Carolina Girl, 54

Tawny Treasure, 26
EFFIE'S PAPA BEAR, 10 Doc's Bay Dream, 8 Pony Girl's Bliss, 228

Thetis, 260
Henry's Hidalgo, 70 Shy Anne, 88

Thunderstorm Skies, 270
A Splash of Freckles, 102 Archer's Gambit, 246 Lorna Dune, 302 Poco's Starry Night, 122 Sonny's Legacy, 262

Tidewater Treasure, 170
JABATAA, 172 Lefty's Checkmark, 218 Susana, 178 Suzy's Sweetheart, 180 Tuleta Star, 182 Tiger Lily, 226

Close Family Index

Tiger Lily, 226
JABATAA, 172 Lefty's Checkmark, 218 Susana, 178 **Suzy's Sweetheart**, 180 Tidewater Treasure, 170 Tuleta Star, 182

Too Grand, 150
Kachina Grand Star, 152 **Daisey**, 6 Ella of Assateague, 38 Molly's Rosebud, 156

Tornado's Legacy, 164
Unci, 20 Bling Bling, 30 CLG ToMorrow's Tidewater Twist, 162 Jigsaw's Little Miss Skeeter, 296 Mary Read, 258 Jessica's Sea Star Sandy, 140 Landrie's Georgia Peach, 142 Precious Jewel, 190 Tornado's Prince of Tides, 288

Tornado's Prince of Tides, 288
Badabing, 160 CLG Bay Princess, 158 Cody's Little Jigsaw Puzzle, 40 Judy's Sunshine, 290 Little Miss Sunshine, 292 Marina's Marsh Mallow, 300 Randy, 166 Jessica's Sea Star Sandy, 140 Landrie's Georgia Peach, 142 Tornado's Legacy, 164

Tuleta Star, 182
JABATAA, 172 Lefty's Checkmark, 218 Susana, 178 Suzy's Sweetheart, 180 Tidewater Treasure, 170 Tiger Lily, 226

Tunie, 52
Don Leonard Stud II, 256 Seaside Miracle, 100

Two Teague's Golden Girl, 282
Chief Golden Eagle, 276 Two Teagues Taco, 18 Chili, 214 CLG Cowboy Kisses, 274 Shy & Sassy Sweet Lady Suede, 280

Two Teagues Taco, 18
Two Teague's Golden Girl, 282 Babe, 60 **Bay Girl**, 4 Black Star, 84 Got Milk, 106 Slash of White, 216 **White Saddle**, 44

Unci, 20
Precious Jewel, 190 Tornado's Legacy, 164

Unforgettable 2001, 192
Bling Bling, 30 Carol's Little Freedom, 50 **Wild Thing**, 78

Wendy's Carolina Girl, 54
Maverick, 104 Talia/Evan's Angel, 112 Serendipity, 168

Whisper of Living Legend, 294
CLG Rumor Has It, 272 *Alice's Sandcastle*, 136 *Archer's Gambit*, 246 *CJ SAMM'N*, 220 *Fifteen Friends of Freckles*, 90 *Gidget's Beach Baby*, 264 *Kachina Grand Star*, 152 *Kimball's Rainbow Delight*, 222 *Little Duckie*, 240

White Saddle, 44
Babe, 60 *Bay Girl*, 4 *Black Star*, 84 *Got Milk*, 106 *Slash of White*, 216 *Two Teagues Taco*, 18

Wild Thing, 78
Splash, 72 Doctor Amrien, 42 Grandma's Dream, 74 Henry's Hidalgo, 70 Ken, 204 Loveland's Secret Feather, 76 Maverick, 104 Skylark, 92 *Carol's Little Freedom*, 50 *Unforgettable 2001*, 192

Wildest Dreams, 82
May's Grand Slam, 48 *Millennium Midnight*, 62 *Miracle's Natural Beauty*, 46 *Seaside Miracle*, 100 *Summer Breeze*, 36

Wildfire, 266
Beach Boy, 134 *Calendar Girl*, 132 *Summer*, 98 *Sundance*, 298

Winter Moon, 96

Witch Kraft, 268
Maverick, 104 *Got Milk*, 106

A

A Splash of Freckles, bay pinto, 102
Ace *see* Ace's Black Tie Affair
Ace's Black Tie Affair, black pinto, 120
Ajax, bay pinto, 56
Alice's Sandcastle, buckskin, 136
Angel *see* Jean Bonde's Bayside Angel
Anna *see* Got Milk
Anne Bonny, chestnut pinto, 236
Archer's Gambit, chestnut pinto, 246

B

Babe, bay pinto, 60
Baby *see* Baybe
Badabing, buckskin pinto, 160
Bay Girl, bay,   4
Bay Princess *see* CLG Bay Princess
Baybe, black pinto, 130
Beach Baby *see* Gidget's Beach Baby
Beach Boy, black pinto, 134
Beach Bunny, chestnut pinto, 244
Black Pearl, black pinto, 128
Black Star, bay pinto, 84
Bling Bling, bay, 30
Blue *see* CLG Surfer's Blue Moon
Blue Moon *see* CLG Surfer's Blue Moon
Breezy *see* Summer Breeze
Butterfly *see* Lefty's Checkmark

C

Calendar Girl, black pinto, 132
Carli Marie, chestnut pinto, 234
Carol's Little Freedom, bay pinto, 50
Carolina Girl *see* Wendy's Carolina Girl
Cash *see* Poco's Starry Night
Catwalk Chaos, chestnut pinto, 232
Catwalk's Olympic Glory, chestnut pinto, 212

Cee Cee *see* Summer Breeze
Checkers, chestnut pinto, 248
Chickadee, bay pinto, 80
Chief *see* Chief Golden Eagle
Chief Golden Eagle, palomino, 276
Chili, chestnut pinto, 214
Cinnamon Blaze, chestnut, 184
CJ SAMM'N, chestnut pinto, 220
CLG Bay Princess, buckskin pinto, 158
CLG Cowboy Kisses, palomino, 274
CLG Ember, black, 110
CLG Rumor Has It, chestnut pinto, 272
CLG Surfer's Blue Moon, black, 116
CLG ToMorrow's Tidewater Twist, buckskin pinto, 162
Cody *see* Dakota Sky's Cody Two Socks
Cody's Little Jigsaw Puzzle, bay pinto, 40
Courtney's Island Dove, chestnut pinto, 252
Cowboy Kisses *see* CLG Cowboy Kisses

D
Daisey, bay, 6
Dakota *see* Stevenson's Dakota Sky
Dakota Sky *see* Stevenson's Dakota Sky
Dakota Sky's Cody Two Socks, bay, 28
Danny's Girl *see* Splash
Destiny *see* Destiny Feathering Spirit
Destiny Feathering Spirit, bay pinto, 66
Diamond *see* Unforgettable 2001
Doc *see* Doctor Amrien
Doc's Bay Dream, bay, 8
Doctor Amrien, bay pinto, 42
Don Leonard Stud II, chestnut pinto, 256
Dove *see* Courtney's Island Dove
Dreamer's Gift, chestnut, 198
Dreamer's Stardust, chestnut, 206
Duckie *see* Sweet Jane

E
Effie's Papa Bear, bay, 10
Ella *see* Ella of Assateague
Ella of Assateague, bay pinto, 38
Ember *see* CLG Ember
ET *see* Scotty ET
Evan's Angel *see* Talia/Evan's Angel

F
Feather *see* Loveland's Secret Feather
Fifteen Friends of Freckles, bay pinto, 90
Fluffy *see* Bay Girl
Freckles *see* Fifteen Friends of Freckles
Friendly Girl *see* Witch Kraft

G
Georgia Peach *see* Landrie's Georgia Peach
Gidget *see* Surfer Dude's Gidget
Gidget's Beach Baby, chestnut pinto, 264
Gingersnap *see* Surfer's Shining Star
Giraffe *see* Checkers
Glory *see* Catwalk's Olympic Glory
Goldie *see* Two Teague's Golden Girl
Good Ole Days Bailey's Star, chestnut pinto, 224
Got Milk, bay pinto, 106
Gracey, black pinto, 126
Grandma's Dream, bay pinto, 74

H
Half n Half *see* Shy Anne
Heide's Sky, bay pinto, 108
Henry's Hidalgo, bay pinto, 70
Hoppy *see* Effie's Papa Bear

I
Ivana Marie Zustan, buckskin, 138

J
JABATAA, chestnut, 172

Jean Bonde's Bayside Angel, bay, 22
Jessica's Sandy *see* Jessica's Sea Star Sandy
Jessica's Sea Star Sandy, buckskin, 140
Jigsaw *see* Cody's Little Jigsaw Puzzle
Jigsaw's Little Miss Skeeter, palomino pinto, 296
Joansie *see* Little Bit O' Joansie
Judy's Little Smooch, chestnut, 194
Judy's Sunshine, palomino pinto, 290

K

Kachina *see* Kachina Grand Star
Kachina Grand Star, buckskin, 152
Kachina Mayli Mist, palomino, 278
Ken, chestnut, 204
Kimball's Rainbow Delight, chestnut pinto, 222
Kimmee-Sue, chestnut, 186

L

Lady *see* Pony Ladies' Sweet Surprise
Lady Hook *see* Susie Q
Landrie's Georgia Peach, buckskin, 142
Leah's Bayside Angel, bay, 24
Lefty's Checkmark, chestnut pinto, 218
Legacy *see* Tornado's Legacy
Lenny *see* Don Leonard Stud II
Leonard Stud II *see* Don Leonard Stud II
Lil Miss Hot Stuff *see* Chili
Lil Tornado *see* Tornado's Legacy
Little Bit O' Joansie, chestnut pinto, 254
Little Dolphin, bay, 12
Little Duckie, chestnut pinto, 240
Little Freedom *see* Carol's Little Freedom
Little Frog *see* Archer's Gambit
Little Miss Sunshine, palomino pinto, 292
Liz's Serenity, buckskin, 144
Lorna Dune, palomino pinto, 302
Loveland's Secret Feather, bay pinto, 76

Alphabetical Index

M

Margarita *see* Catwalk Chaos
Marguerite of Chincoteague, bay pinto, 86
Marina's Marsh Mallow, palomino pinto, 300
Marsh Mallow *see* Marina's Marsh Mallow
Mary Read, chestnut pinto, 258
Maverick, bay pinto, 104
May *see* May's Grand Slam
May's Grand Slam, bay pinto, 48
Mayli *see* Kachina Mayli Mist
Millennium Midnight, bay pinto, 62
Milly Sue, black, 114
Miracle's Natural Beauty, bay pinto, 46
Miss Admiral Halsey, palomino, 284
MissMe, bay pinto, 58
Misty Mills, chestnut pinto, 242
Molly's Rosebud, buckskin pinto, 156
Moon *see* Winter Moon

N

Napolean *see* Rainbow Warrior
Natural Beauty *see* Miracle's Natural Beauty
Neptune *see* Little Dolphin

O

Oreo *see* Millennium Midnight

P

Pappy's Pony, bay, 14
Pearl *see* Black Pearl
Pixie Dust, black pinto, 124
Poco Latte PW, buckskin, 146
Poco's Starry Night, black pinto, 122
Pony Girl's Bliss, chestnut pinto, 228
Pony Ladies' Sweet Surprise, bay, 16
Poseidon's Fury *see* Effie's Papa Bear
Precious Jewel, chestnut, 190
Prince *see* Tornado's Prince of Tides

Puzzle *see* Archer's Gambit

Q
Quackers *see* Little Duckie
Queenie *see* Tunie

R
Rainbow Delight *see* Kimball's Rainbow Delight
Rainbow Warrior, bay pinto, 64
Rainy *see* Kimball's Rainbow Delight
Randy, buckskin pinto, 166
Renegade *see* Beach Boy
Riptide *see* Surfer's Riptide
Rosie *see* Molly's Rosebud
Rosie's Teapot, bay pinto, 34
Rumor *see* CLG Rumor Has It

S
Salt Water Taffee *see* Too Grand
Saltwater Renegade *see* Beach Boy
Scarlet *see* Surfin' Scarlet
Scotty ET, bay pinto, 94
Seaside Miracle, bay pinto, 100
Secret *see* Loveland's Secret Feather
Serendipity, buckskin pinto, 168
Shy & Sassy Sweet Lady Suede, palomino, 280
Shy Anne, bay pinto, 88
Skeeter *see* Jigsaw's Little Miss Skeeter
Skylark, bay pinto, 92
Slash of White, chestnut pinto, 216
Smooch *see* Judy's Little Smooch
Sonny's Legacy, chestnut pinto, 262
Splash, bay pinto, 72
Splash of Freckles *see* A Splash of Freckles
Star *see* Good Ole Days Bailey's Star
Stardust *see* Dreamer's Stardust
Starry Night *see* Poco's Starry Night
Stevenson's Dakota Sky, chestnut pinto, 250

Suede *see* Shy & Sassy Sweet Lady Suede
Summer, bay pinto, 98
Summer Breeze, bay pinto, 36
Sundance, palomino pinto, 298
Sunny *see* Sunrise Ocean Tides
Sunrise Ocean Tides, buckskin, 148
Sunshine *see* Little Miss Sunshine
Surfer Dude's Gidget, chestnut, 196
Surfer Princess, chestnut, 200
Surfer's Blue Moon *see* CLG Surfer's Blue Moon
Surfer's Riptide, chestnut, 208
Surfer's Shining Star, chestnut, 174
Surfette, chestnut, 202
Surfin' Chantel, chestnut, 176
Surfin' Scarlet, chestnut, 188
Susana, chestnut, 178
Susie Q, chestnut pinto, 230
Suzy's Sweetheart, chestnut, 180
Sweet Jane, chestnut pinto, 238
Sweetheart, bay pinto, 68

T
Taco *see* Two Teagues Taco
Talia *see* Talia/Evan's Angel
Talia/Evan's Angel, black, 112
Tawny Treasure, bay, 26
Thetis, chestnut pinto, 260
Thunder *see* Thunderstorm Skies
Thunderstorm Skies, chestnut pinto, 270
Tidewater Treasure, buckskin pinto, 170
Tidewater Twist *see* CLG ToMorrow's Tidewater Twist
Tiger Lily, chestnut pinto, 226
Too Grand, buckskin, 150
Tornado's Legacy, buckskin pinto, 164
Tornado's Prince of Tides, palomino pinto, 288
Treasure *see* Tidewater Treasure

Triple T *see* CLG ToMorrow's Tidewater Twist
Tuleta Star, chestnut, 182
Tunie, bay pinto, 52
Twist *see* CLG ToMorrow's Tidewater Twist
Two Teague's Golden Girl, palomino, 282
Two Teagues Taco, bay, 18

U
Unci, bay, 20
Unforgettable 2001, chestnut, 192

V
Valentine *see* Ken

W
Waterbaby *see* Tiger Lily
Wendy's Carolina Girl, bay pinto, 54
Whisper *see* Whisper of Living Legend
Whisper of Living Legend, palomino pinto, 294
White Saddle, bay pinto, 44
Wild Thing, bay pinto, 78
Wildest Dreams, bay pinto, 82
Wildfire, chestnut pinto, 266
Wings *see* Judy's Sunshine
Winter Moon, bay pinto, 96
Witch Kraft, chestnut pinto, 268

Z
Zustan *see* Ivana Marie Zustan

Stallion Index

Bay
Effie's Papa Bear, 10
Little Dolphin, 12

Bay Pinto
Ajax, 56
Henry's Hidalgo, 70
Maverick, 104
Rainbow Warrior, 64
Wild Thing, 78

Black Pinto
Ace's Black Tie Affair, 120
Beach Boy, 134

Buckskin Pinto
CLG ToMorrow's Tidewater Twist, 162
Tornado's Legacy, 164

Chestnut
Ken, 204
Surfer's Riptide, 208

Chestnut Pinto
Archer's Gambit, 246
Don Leonard Stud II, 256

Palomino
Chief Golden Eagle, 276

Palomino Pinto
Tornado's Prince of Tides, 288

00
Ella of Assateague, bay pinto, 38
Surfin' Scarlet, chestnut, 188
Too Grand, buckskin, 150
Whisper of Living Legend, palomino pinto, 294

01
Stevenson's Dakota Sky, chestnut pinto, 250
Susana, chestnut, 178
Thetis, chestnut pinto, 260

02
JABATAA, chestnut, 172
Poco Latte PW, buckskin, 146
Scotty ET, bay pinto, 94
Surfer Dude's Gidget, chestnut, 196
Tuleta Star, chestnut, 182

03
Pappy's Pony, bay, 14
Tunie, bay pinto, 52

04
Landrie's Georgia Peach, buckskin, 142
Pony Ladies' Sweet Surprise, bay, 16

05
Dakota Sky's Cody Two Socks, bay, 28
Kachina Grand Star, buckskin, 152
Two Teagues Taco, bay, 18

06
CJ SAMM'N, chestnut pinto, 220
Fifteen Friends of Freckles, bay pinto, 90
Jessica's Sea Star Sandy, buckskin, 140
Kimball's Rainbow Delight, chestnut pinto, 222
Misty Mills, chestnut pinto, 242
Sweet Jane, chestnut pinto, 238

Brand Index

07
Ace's Black Tie Affair, black pinto, 120
Ajax, bay pinto, 56
Effie's Papa Bear, bay, 10
Tornado's Legacy, buckskin pinto, 164
Tornado's Prince of Tides, palomino pinto, 288

08
Archer's Gambit, chestnut pinto, 246
Chief Golden Eagle, palomino, 276
Ken, chestnut, 204
Little Dolphin, bay, 12
Wildest Dreams, bay pinto, 82

09
Miracle's Natural Beauty, bay pinto, 46
Surfer's Riptide, chestnut, 208

12
Alice's Sandcastle, buckskin, 136
Dreamer's Gift, chestnut, 198
Kachina Mayli Mist, palomino, 278
Kimmee-Sue, chestnut, 186
Loveland's Secret Feather, bay pinto, 76
May's Grand Slam, bay pinto, 48
Poco's Starry Night, black pinto, 122

13
Chickadee, bay pinto, 80
Cody's Little Jigsaw Puzzle, bay pinto, 40
Gracey, black pinto, 126
Grandma's Dream, bay pinto, 74
Lorna Dune, palomino pinto, 302
Marguerite of Chincoteague, bay pinto, 86
Rosie's Teapot, bay pinto, 34
Sonny's Legacy, chestnut pinto, 262
Surfin' Chantel, chestnut, 176
Thunderstorm Skies, chestnut pinto, 270
White Saddle, bay pinto, 44

14

Black Pearl, black pinto, 128
Doctor Amrien, bay pinto, 42
Don Leonard Stud II, chestnut pinto, 256
Little Bit O' Joansie, chestnut pinto, 254
Marina's Marsh Mallow, palomino pinto, 300
Maverick, bay pinto, 104
Pixie Dust, black pinto, 124
Precious Jewel, chestnut, 190
Randy, buckskin pinto, 166
Shy & Sassy Sweet Lady Suede, palomino, 280
Splash, bay pinto, 72

15

Badabing, buckskin pinto, 160
Beach Boy, black pinto, 134
Beach Bunny, chestnut pinto, 244
Bling Bling, bay, 30
CLG Surfer's Blue Moon, black, 116
Jean Bonde's Bayside Angel, bay, 22
Little Miss Sunshine, palomino pinto, 292
Sunrise Ocean Tides, buckskin, 148
Surfer Princess, chestnut, 200
Surfer's Shining Star, chestnut, 174

16

Catwalk's Olympic Glory, chestnut pinto, 212
CLG Bay Princess, buckskin pinto, 158
Ivana Marie Zustan, buckskin, 138
Two Teague's Golden Girl, palomino, 282

17

Calendar Girl, black pinto, 132
Chili, chestnut pinto, 214
CLG Cowboy Kisses, palomino, 274
CLG ToMorrow's Tidewater Twist, buckskin pinto, 162
Henry's Hidalgo, bay pinto, 70
Liz's Serenity, buckskin, 144

Brand Index

Mary Read, chestnut pinto, 258
Milly Sue, black, 114
MissMe, bay pinto, 58
Pony Girl's Bliss, chestnut pinto, 228
Surfette, chestnut, 202
Talia/Evan's Angel, black, 112
Tawny Treasure, bay, 26

18

Carli Marie, chestnut pinto, 234
CLG Ember, black, 110
CLG Rumor Has It, chestnut pinto, 272
Doc's Bay Dream, bay, 8
Dreamer's Stardust, chestnut, 206
Jigsaw's Little Miss Skeeter, palomino pinto, 296
Judy's Sunshine, palomino pinto, 290
Miss Admiral Halsey, palomino, 284
Serendipity, buckskin pinto, 168
Wendy's Carolina Girl, bay pinto, 54

7

Checkers, chestnut pinto, 248

94

Babe, bay pinto, 60

96

Susie Q, chestnut pinto, 230

98

Slash of White, chestnut pinto, 216
Suzy's Sweetheart, chestnut, 180

99

Carol's Little Freedom, bay pinto, 50

F

Little Duckie, chestnut pinto, 240
Seaside Miracle, bay pinto, 100
Surfer Dude's Gidget, chestnut, 196

Thunderbolt

stallion   brand: none
CHIEF GOLDEN EAGLE X BLING BLING

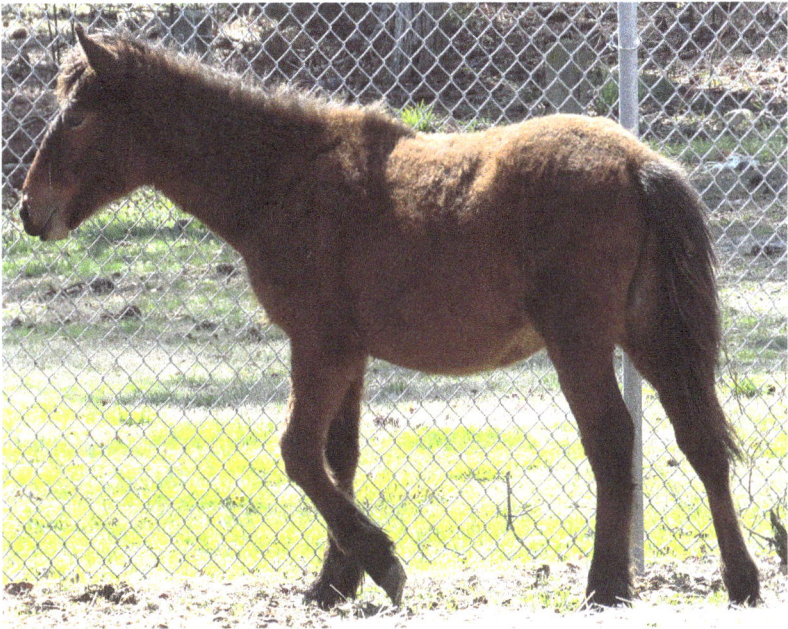

Close Family Members
CHIEF GOLDEN EAGLE, 276 BLING BLING, 30 *Chili*, 214
CLG Cowboy Kisses, 274 *Shy & Sassy Sweet Lady Suede*, 280
Two Teague's Golden Girl, 282

NOTE: By the time I became aware that Thunderbolt was staying with the herd, this book was completely finished and ready for publication. Rather than leave him out, I decided to stuff him in the back.

www.ingramcontent.com/pod-product-compliance
Lightning Source LLC
Chambersburg PA
CBHW041255040426
42334CB00028BA/3018